T
LITTLE THINGS
THAT CAN MAKE A
BIG
DIFFERENCE
IN YOUR
MARRIAGE

What They Don't Tell You Before
You Get Married

DR SOLA FOLA-ALADE

THE LITTLE THINGS THAT CAN MAKE A BIG DIFFERENCE IN YOUR MARRIAGE

Copyright © Dr Sola Fola-Alade 2010

ISBN:978-0-9564-767-0-8

Published by Vision Media Comm. Ltd
Email: info@colourdesigns.co.uk Tel: +44 7903 822 987

Printed in United Kingdom

ENDORSEMENTS

This book is rich, because of Sola's wealth of experience. His many years as a pastor, counsellor, and a passion for writing; a great marriage to his wife Bimbo, his personal experiences, a successful marriage ministry and a commitment to building godly marriages qualify him to speak and write about the institution of marriage. Tap into a rich vein as you read.

Agu Irukwu
RCCG Jesus House, London, U.K

This is not just another book on marriage. Things are changing and at a very fast rate. Change is here, with a massive erosion of values. It is happening unconsciously but surely. Dr Sola Fola-Alade understands the dynamics and the impact on our marriages. Let's save our homes, and our society. Every wise man or woman must digest and act on the contents of this book.

Sam Adeyemi
Daystar Christian Centre, Nigeria

This book is a lifesaver. It is factual and functional in every dimension of marriage. The guidelines and instruction generously splashed in the content by the author, Dr. Sola Fola-Alade, will equip you for successful marriage. As a medical doctor, the author has released a tool for the prevention and treatment of chronic marriage diseases. Save your life and marriage by immersing yourself in these priceless pages of captivating insight.

"Take us the foxes, the little foxes, that spoil the vines: for our vines have tender grapes." Song of Solomon 2:15

Eastwood Anaba
Fountain Gate Ministries, Ghana

Little things can make a big impact on your marriage not after the book but even as you turn each page. This is a great little book to give you a big bang in your daily work with your spouse. This is one precious jewel every marriage needs to make your marriage shine. Wisdom, guidance, and really practical advice characterises this book with big ideas about the little things.

Douglas Weiss Phd
Marriage Counsellor & Sex therapist
Heart to Heart Counselling, Colorado Springs, USA

ACKNOWLEDGEMENTS

I would like to appreciate & acknowledge the efforts of Bimpe Ogunleye, Toyin Kayode, Tola Jegede, Vona Aghoghovbia & Chuks Mbatogu who all helped in their various ways towards making this book an editorial success.

I also want to thank Tokunbo Emmanuel, Bisi Popoola & Taiwo Sofowora for helping out with editing and proof reading work. Thanks to Bayo Awe and the Vision Media Communications team for project managing the publishing of the book. A very big thank you to Tunde Adewumi for helping co-ordinate all our efforts & for your relentless dedication to God & his work & your loyalty over the last 14 years, you are a true example of enduring fruit. And of course lots of appreciation to my lovely wife of many years for allowing me to write this book amidst all the chaos & the vicissitudes that life throws daily & also for giving up of your time and sleep to help reword & rearrange the book to make this book readable. We really wrote this book together. Abimbola you are simply the best.

A great big "Thank You" to everyone that has been involved from start to finish.

DEDICATION

This book is dedicated to my lovely wife Abimbola Rebecca Fola-Alade for her tremendous dedication as a highly valued & multi-varied wife, a devoted mother & selfless Pastor. She is simply a "Super-Woman" one who daily lives out an extraordinary life in a very simple & ordinary way. She continues to impact and influence the lives of thousands either through a thought provoking message or via TV and various other forms of media. She holds our home together by her phenomenal home management skills and as she carefully guides the path of tomorrow's leaders (our sons) today. She is really a Proverbs 31 woman in 21st century times, seeking to live out the timeless truths of scripture in changing times with shifting values.

The writer of Proverbs articulates the thoughts of my heart when he said in Proverbs 31:27-30 that:
" 27 She watches over the ways of her household,
And does not eat the bread of idleness.
28 Her children rise up and call her blessed;
Her husband also, and he praises her:
29 " Many daughters have done well,
But you excel them all."
30 Charm is deceitful and beauty is passing,
But a woman who fears the LORD, she shall be praised."

She is Simply, Sweet, Simple but Sophisticated. It is the little things she does that has made the big difference in my life & ministry. She continually adds value to everything she touches and does.

Abimbola,
You are truly loved & appreciated. My love is for a lifetime.

FOREWORD

One of the things that drew me to my husband was the testimony of a married woman on how his counsel has transformed her life and marriage. She informed me that she had called on him to settle a dispute between her and her husband (who sometimes hit her during disagreements). On hearing the full facts of the current argument, my husband invited the husband to come on a drive with him to clear the air and talk. She said what they talked about remains a mystery (the husband never told her what they talked about) but she didn't mind because since they took that drive several years had elapsed and her husband had never hit her again. Interestingly, all this had happened when my husband was single and had no marital experience!

Now having been married over a decade and with many more years of experience helping couples relationally, he has a lot more to share – from his personal experience and from his role as a pastor. Over the years of our marriage, through good and bad times, I have observed him work at applying biblical principles as he strives to be an excellent husband and father to our children. He is sensitive to the promptings of the Spirit, quick to apologise when wrong, affectionate, generous, able to lead and to take counsel. He has and continues to be my best friend, my lover, my pastor and a loving father to my children.

This book is a must read for all those who are serious about building a quality marriage. Few of us realise when we get married, how much it's going to require of us – how much we'll have to change, adapt and persevere. We are not often aware of what the seasons of life will throw at us or the hard work required to stay together for a lifetime and enjoy it. From the first blush of romance to the excitement of the wedding day, and on through the pains of learning to live together and handle tough times- in this book, each season of married life is analysed. We learn what challenges we can anticipate, how to deal with them and build marriages that will stand the test of time.

You will learn
- How to search for a partner if you are ready for marriage
- What to look for in a mate
- Common marital issues and problems
- What makes a marriage lose its lustre
- What makes a spouse vulnerable to adultery
- How to fall in love again with your spouse
- How to keep your marriage strong and vital

The author, my husband, has by the way he lives out his life as a husband and father, deemed himself highly qualified to write this book. I heartily recommend this book to you – it will make your marriage stronger. Enjoy!

Bimbo Fola-Alade

PREFACE

DO YOU HAVE WHAT IT TAKES TO MAKE YOUR MARRIAGE WORK?

IF MARRIAGE IS SO GOOD, WHY ARE THEY ASKING FOR A DIVORCE?

When I finally decided to write this book, it felt like I was literally dragged by God to my writing desk to give voice to an issue that broke His heart. After almost two decades of ministry and counselling, I can confidently say I have seen the good, bad and ugly and almost everything in between about relationships. I have witnessed a common pattern in dating and marital relationships. Many couples in dating relationships have come to see my wife and I, feeling ecstatic, elated and euphoric about their future. Sadly, after a few years, the same wildly-in-love couple now desperately want to take the fire exit out of a very bitter and acrimonious marriage; cussing and inflicting maximum pain on each other. What happened to these couples after the wedding? If marriage is so good, why are so many people asking for a divorce?

"If marriage is so good, why do my parents want a divorce?"

We live in a broken society. Approximately 50% of marriages end up in divorce; and as a result we are seeing more children from broken homes than ever before. Marriages are breaking up and society is deteriorating as a result. Statistics make it clear that children from broken homes are more likely to get involved in crime, perform poorly at school, develop psychological and social problems, have unwanted pregnancies and get hooked on drugs.- ref. It is because of this kind of societal fragmentation that God stirred up the "Weeping Prophet", Jeremiah, to wail over Israel. God was perturbed by the state of the nation, and saddened by the lethargy and inertia of those who had the power, position and means to do something about it. He was so burdened that He raised a prophet who would not only speak to the ills in the nation, but also proffer lasting solutions to address the issues. God declared by the prophet Jeremiah:

"Everyone's after the dishonest dollar,
little people and big people alike.
Prophets and priests and everyone in between
twist words and doctor truth.
My dear Daughter—my people—broken, shattered,
and yet they put on Band-Aids,
Saying, "It's not so bad. You'll be just fine."
But things are not "just fine"! The crops are in, the summer is over,
but for us nothing's changed.
We're still waiting to be rescued.
For my dear broken people, I'm heartbroken.
I weep, seized by grief.
Are there no healing ointments in Gilead?

Isn't there a doctor in the house?
So why can't something be done
to heal and save my dear, dear people?"
Jeremiah 8:11, 22.

I believe each one of us has a part to play in mending and healing society's wounds; one way we can do this is by ensuring that we avoid adding to the problem. This we can do by building better and lasting marriages. It has been said that, "If we fail to build better marriages, we will have to build bigger prisons."-ref. It is my conclusion, after two decades of counselling couples, that marriage, like anything else in life, works and succeeds on the practise of a few principles. These principles I am calling "the little things", which if neglected will result in big damage or if understood and applied will make a "big difference" in any marriage.

"The little things", which if neglected will result in big damage or if understood and applied will make a "Big difference" in any marriage."

It is the little things that make a big difference between the marriages that succeed and those that don't. Little things like taking a pre-marital course and asking the right questions can go a long way in laying enduring foundations for a marriage. Other little things matter, like going on regular dates once married and practising acts of kindness after signing on the dotted lines also make a big difference. Come along with me and discover the little things that will make a big difference in your marriage.

This book is written in three parts covering the following themes:

PART ONE
THE PREPARATION FOR MARRIAGE

DEVELOPING WHAT IT TAKES TO MAKE A MARRIAGE WORK

PART TWO
THE PROBLEMS IN MARRIAGE

IDENTIFYING THE BAD THINGS THAT DESTROY GOOD MARRIAGES

PART THREE
THE PLEASURES IN MARRIAGE

HOW TO ALWAYS ENJOY BEING MARRIED

If you take the time and effort to learn and apply the principles in the following pages, I restate- **the little improvements you make will make a big difference in your marriage**.

Enjoy the read.
Dr.Sola Fola-Alade

CONTENT

PART ONE

PREPARATION FOR MARRIAGE

CHAPTER 1

BREAKING HOMES

Only a few days into the year 2010, the nation of Haiti was hit by one of the most devastating earthquakes the world has ever witnessed. The earthquake was so bad that even the Presidential Palace and the United Nations building did not survive it. Very few buildings were standing tall and strong after the incident. Those that survived perhaps had unusually fortified foundations and structures which were incorporated into the design at the pre-building stage.

In a similar light, few marriages will survive the storms of the challenges and evil in today's society if they are not built intentionally and intelligently.

Marriages are under constant attack. The home front is under a direct and constant assault from the enemy. Some years ago, 2,500 Satanists were reported to have come together in Pretoria, South Africa to curse marriages. If Satanists take praying against marriages seriously, Christians need to wake up and take strong action to build their marriages. Some people struggle to fast for their marriages, yet Satanists rise up to curse good marriages. Even without the curse and without Satanists, marriages are degenerating and disintegrating, because of prevalent societal mores.

> ## "Very few buildings were seen standing tall & strong after the incident. Those that survived perhaps had unusual fortified foundations & structures which were incorporated into the design at the pre-building."

In Noah's days, God looked down and saw that the earth was corrupt and filled with violence. That word 'corrupt' here, means changing from good to bad or 'to *degrade with unsound principles or moral values.'* The world has changed in morals, manners and values. And current cultural values of self-fulfilment, experimentation and multiple coupling do not support marriage. Talk shows on Television define marriage in a perverted way, eroding the biblical foundational principles of marriage. Today, two men or two women can get married. Even in church the sound principles that undergird the foundations of marriage is distorted. Many single people in the church are sexually active. Divorce is also commonplace among church goers; and about 50 percent of married churchgoers have been involved in extramarital affairs. This is recorded data which does not include those that are involved in affairs in their hearts (inordinate affection). What has happened to God's ordained institution?

"Some years back, 2,500 Satanists were reported to have come together in Pretoria, South Africa to curse marriages."

Because marriages have deteriorated, what used to be known as a good and enviable institution is now discredited and dreaded - fewer people are getting married and staying married. Many people do not plan to ever marry. This may be because their parents had a traumatic marriage which did not work out; that they do not see themselves having a successful marriage because they haven't seen any. For many people, marriage holds negative memories. This shows evidently that the institution has been corrupted.

What we see today is a total mess therefore we need a remedy and hope. Prayer is the key (especially with evidence that the devil is raising direct attacks on marriage). We need to pray, but more importantly, we need to get wisdom. Wisdom is the revealed will of God. It is insight from God and following God's patterns. The only homes, marriages or houses that will stand the storms and vicissitudes of life are the ones founded upon the revelation of God. There are so many challenges in life today that you need extra reinforcement to stand against the enemy's wiles.

The Amplified Bible better elaborates this text in Proverbs 24.

"Through skilful and godly Wisdom is a house (a life, a home, a family) built, and by understanding it is established [on a sound and good foundation], and by knowledge shall its chambers [of every area] be filled with all precious and pleasant riches" (Proverbs 24: 3-4 *Amp*).

God is concerned about the corruption of marriage. This was why He spoke to Noah, saying that He was appalled by the state of affairs on the earth and the level of corruption. He was looking for a remnant, a few people who would be different for Him. Can you be different for God? Will you decide to stand out?

MARRIAGE CERTIFICATE VERSUS DRIVER'S LICENCE

Marriage is the only institution I know of that gives its members' certificates before they sit for tests. This is unlike the procedure of entry to most institutions. With school or university for example, you have to apply, get your application approved with specified requirements for entry. You then have to sit classes, prepare for and pass exams at the specified grade to gain entry to the school or university. With marriage however, you simply turn up say 'I do', give and receive a ring, then a certificate is given to you – you are now officially part of the marriage club. Then the tests begin- the test of living together harmoniously with someone so different from you in many ways. Perhaps this is why there are so many more marital accidents than road traffic accidents. No one will give you the keys to a car without adequate preparation, but they'll give you the key to someone else's life based on feelings - Its pure madness!

So many people enter marriage without adequate preparation; many have no clue what they are getting into. Most people assume that what they learnt at the beauty salon or at the barber's shop is sufficient. Some people don't even know much about how the opposite sex ticks before they get married. I had the privilege to learn about the anatomy and physiology of a woman for seven years as part of my study in

Medical School so I understood how my wife's body works even before I met her. Many women don't understand what drives a man and how he process's his thoughts and some men don't understand that a woman's mood changes with cyclical events. A lot of men think that they have it together - until you ask their wives. Before you get married you need to know what you are getting into – who you will be living with and what makes them tick. You need to understand how the mind and body of your spouse works, as well as the impact of gender, personality and background differences.

WILL YOUR MARRIAGE SATISFY THE BUILDING CODE?

Do you remember the story about the three little pigs? Each pig built a house with different materials. One built with straw, the other with sticks, and the last with stones, and then a wolf came by. They had built without knowing that a wolf would come. The Bible says that the enemy comes as a roaring lion, seeking whom to devour. You know how it ends and which house was standing after the visit.

"Theses pigs all built three different houses with different materials. One built with straw, the other with sticks, and the last with stones and then a wolf came by. These people built without knowing that a wolf would come."

A lot of us build our homes and marriages without knowing that the enemy (like the wolf) will huff and puff, and try to blow our houses down. Some marriages are built with faulty materials like emotions (he 'Oh, he's so cute' crew). Yet others build with wrong motives (because they are over 30 and their contemporaries are getting married) or due to parental pressures some give in to pre-arranged marriages out of desperation. So they get married and build their marriage out of straw. They have a ring on their finger but when the wolf huffs and puffs and blows, the house comes crashing down. I pray that you will refuse to be manipulated, rushed, or forced into choices that won't last. Decide to build right: wait for God, hear Him and follow God's precise pattern and plan for your life. These are those who build on the rock.

If you are going to build right, you need to have the right foundation laid by God. Noah had never seen rain before but he still prepared for the rain by obeying God's precise pattern. Many bachelors and spinsters don't listen to guidance because they have never seen marital rain or flood hit a house. They say they love each other and believe such things cannot happen to them.

If you want a marriage that will withstand the storms, you need to prepare and build according to God's pattern in this order:

- Knowing and choosing God's '**WILL**'

- Doing it God's '**WAY**'

- Doing it '**WHEN**' God's says

I heard it clearly when He said 'this is the one.' I also did it God's way. You need to choose the right person, do it the right way and at God's time. If you have chosen the wrong person already, did it the wrong way and at the wrong time, God can help you. The Bible says in Psalms 11:3 *KJV*, "if the foundations be destroyed, what can the righteous do?" My suggestion is - Pray! But for those who have yet to make the choice, read on. In the next chapter we will talk about knowing God's will (being and choosing the right person); but below lets look at doing it God's way and when He say's so.

GOD'S WAY
CAN YOU OPERATE THIS GADGET?

We once had a TV that had been given to us as a gift. After awhile the power button came off leaving a little hole and the children began stuffing tiny objects into it. Needless to say we could no longer get it to come on. Sometimes we would have to hit or bang it to get it working. Eventually we decided to change it for a plasma TV, but when the new TV arrived it sat there for two weeks because we did not know how to set it up. We had a blessing in our house but did not know how to operate it. We did not have enough understanding to make the most of it.

Many people have similar situations in their marriages. Some husbands think they have to hit their wives (like we had to hit our old TV) to get her to behave properly; some wives treat their husbands like the new TV- they are afraid to touch him because they don't know how he operates. Unfortunately human beings don't come with operating instructions. You have to learn what to press to get the best out of them. Noah's family and all the animals went into the ark, Noah must have had some knowledge that He used to keep all the animals and human beings living together harmoniously. It is not enough to be saved or a Christian. You also need understanding to live with others.

GET WISDOM

"Through wisdom a house is built, And by understanding it is established" (Proverbs 24:3 *NKJV).*

Wisdom will give you a stable foundation and understanding will help you build a strong structure for your marriage. Wisdom is like the architectural plan for the house, telling you the dimensions by which to build. It tells you who to marry, how to marry and when to marry. You need understanding after you have built the foundation. It is with understanding that you build upon that which has been laid through wisdom.

One of the ways you can gain wisdom and understanding is by reading books and listening to audio about marriage, and by submitting yourself to the authority and guidance of more mature people. Over the years, I have noticed that many single people like to hide their relationships; they often choose to keep things secret until they have reached the point of no return. It is not wise - my advice is don't try to hide your relationship from your pastor. Go for pre-marital guidance so that you will not have to go to post marital counselling. As the African proverb goes, "What you hide from your father will be settled by him afterwards". If you don't seek advice beforehand, you will seek advice afterwards. It's better to go for pre-marital counselling so you can be guided aright and given the specifications for building so that you will not have to do damage limitation afterwards. The guidance of more mature Christians is essential to help you know the correctt things to look for in a mate and how to conduct your courtship and prepare for marriage properly. Conduct your courtship in the best and right way.

When you conduct your relationship openly and with a willingness to be corrected and guided by more mature Christian couples – you are showing that you want to do things God's way. Yes people will be in your business – but its to help you, not hurt you.

People will tell you not to have sex with one another; because many of them have suffered from engaging in premarital sex. When my wife asked married women to give one single piece of advice to the single ladies at a seminar once, the response was interesting. Many of the married women said 'Whatever you do, dont sleep with him before marriage'. Many of them were speaking from experience – they knew what it was to deal with the unspoken loss of respect once the deed was done (pre-marriage) and the guilt they struggled with afterwards. Some of them knew that sleeping with each other before marriage was a real dampner on fireworks on the honeymoon. Why? Because they'd done it all already; they had already entered all the rooms in the house – the excitement was gone. Furthermore having done it outside the covenant of marriage, many men who are not strong in the Lord don't appreciate the sacredness and exclusive nature of sex, when its not sizzling at home, some of them look for it with someone else.

MARITAL RAIN

Those advising should also help you to be realistic about what marriage entails. Some single people think marriage is a fulfilled prophecy according to Mills and Boon and when they get married and things begin to look very different from what they expected, disappointment sets in. Many single's do not know that when they see a married couple wearing matching outfits and smiling all may not be as it appears. One pastor told us of a couple in his church who initiated divorce proceedings a few weeks after winning the couple of the year award! They looked great in public but at home they were probably sleeping facing opposite directions due to various storms they were experiencing.

The truth is that just as Noah's ark faced the flood, every marriage faces storms. Whether you build right or not, a storm is coming in different ways. Some face financial storms. Some wives find out that their husband is not as rich as he appeared. All his designer suits and shirts were borrowed and his car, plasma TV and sofa are not yet paid for. They end up in debt and a previously good credit history becomes bad due to association. Some couples face long periods of infertility. Some face years of unemployment or battle ill health. Some people's pre-Christ past catches up with them and they end up in prison or are forced to relocate to another country due to immigration issues. Sometimes when the storms of life come, you find yourself wishing 'the two isn't one.'

Good counsellors will also speak to you about in-laws and how children impact a marriage. I read a book once titled 'Is there is sex after children'! That title should tell you how much children can affect a marriage. Children are God's blessings, but the dynamics of the relationship change when they come. They are demanding, intrusive and time absorbing – prepare for your life to change beyond measure when you have them!

WHEN

It is possible to have started in God's way but rather than date for a good length of time in order to get to know each other and prepare adequately, they rush into marriage. The 'when' is as important as the 'who' and the 'way'. Many marriages struggle, not because the couples are incompatible but because they started wrong- without adequate preparation.

My wife once counselled a couple who hadn't courted for long but were eager to get married. My wife had apprehensions because the couple were so different and they had some peculiar circumstances, the girl was pregnant with a child from a previous relationship. My wife felt they needed to explore their differences more and that the chap had to come to grips about the reality of raising someone else's child. Despite her encouragement to them that they wait, they hurried on ahead. Sadly the marriage didn't last long. It is possible that had they taken time to explore and smooth over their differences, come to an agreement about the rearing of the child and grown in appreciation for each other that they could have had a good marriage. However they weren't willing to put in the time or the work to prepare properly.

A long courtship has several advantages. The main one is that it enables you to see your fiancée for who he or she really is. If you have not had an argument yet, wait till you have one before you get married because it's very revealing and may well bring up other issues you weren't aware of. In marriage you will have conflicts and you need to know how to deal with it before marriage. Some people have a 'take no prisoners' approach in arguments and you may be amazed at the spiteful nature revealed in an argument of someone you had thought of as lovely. Or perhaps it's the considerate and refrained nature revealed in an argument that confirms the godly character of a potential spouse. Storms are bound to come, so you need to know what you will be dealing with in conflict situations in marriage (is your potential mate a whirlwind or a soothing breeze). Its important to get the foundations right.

If you are to spend a lifetime with someone, isn't it worth investing a year or two preparing properly for it?

CHAPTER 2

SO, WILL MARRIAGE MAKE YOU HAPPY?

A number of children were asked what marriage is and they gave some interesting answers. The first one said, "Marriage is when you keep a girl and you don't have to give her back to her parents." The next one explained, "It means spending a lot of time together even if you don't want to" (I think many adults would agree with this definition). The third one said, "It is when two people who have a house and kids decide to take the same name so that other people don't get confused." This is marriage in the eyes of children.

I am sure you chuckled at some of these definitions, thinking how simple their definitions were. Yet surprisingly many adults have very simple ideas about marriage and underestimate what it takes to make a marriage work. You see, we tend to believe fairy tales. We've been raised on stories of Cinderella, Sleeping Beauty, Beauty and the Beast and the likes, such that every young lady is waiting for the prince who will come and kiss her and wake her up from her sleep. Then they drive away in a carriage and live happily ever after.

The fact that we believe these fairy tales is quite evident in our everyday life. Initially, at weddings single ladies lined up eagerly when the bride threw her bouquet; believing the myth that whoever catches the bouquet is the next on the line. Nowadays many don't bother - they have caught so many bouquets and they are still single! After attending a wedding, some single ladies go home depressed, wondering "Why wasn't I the one who got married?" Valentines day is another confirmation of the romantic ideas we have about marriage. A lot of single people feel like they are missing out on something on Valentine's Day. Love always seems to be in the air. Valentine's Day tends to bring joy and elation for those who are courting, but depression for those who aren't. Single people would say the reason for this depression is because they don't have a man or woman to hold. However, married people are perhaps even more depressed than singles are on this lovers' day, because we all believe the same myth - except they have the ingredients for romance, but aren't experiencing it!

WHOEVER THE SHOE FITS WILL MARRY THE PRINCE

Oftentimes, when I believe that God is about to bless me, I take out items from my wardrobe and give them to people who work with me, the guys who I share my time of prayer and life with. I give it to them because I believe if God is going to promote me, I've got to promote other people. There is a particular pair of shoes that I wore for my engagement back in my home country. It was an unusual colour and very nice. I had only worn them twice but I kept them due to sentimental attachment. When I eventually decided to give them out, the young man that I gave it to was in the process of trying it out when I told him, "You're getting married soon." He replied, 'Yes pastor, I feel it…' He got married shortly after that. And that reminded me of the story of Cinderella, "whoever the shoe fits will marry the prince."

I really wish it were truly so, but sadly it is not so in real life is. That is only a fairy tale. The 'happily ever after' of fairly tales is not realistic. I'm not saying that you can't live happily in marriage, but not like they say in the fairy tales. We tend to have this, abstract, romantic view about marriage. In truth marriage does have benefits and blessings, but they are unlike the romantic notions we grow up with. What marriage offers is a lot more concrete and solid.

THE BLESSINGS OF MARRIED LIFE

I remember when I first got married and wore my ring, I felt great. I like it when I see myself in photographs with my ring showing because it looks honourable; I guess that's what Hebrews 13:4 means by saying, "Marriage is honourable and the bed undefiled." Marriage confers an air of responsibility and maturity. In the same way, women like to show off their rings because it tells others "*I belong to someone, I have a protector and I look after a home*'. That's the honour that marriage brings.

After we got married, some close friends of ours picked up my wife and I from the hotel, and on the way home I kept saying 'my wife and I' repeatedly, and one of them said, "Pastor I give you a few months at the most, this wife thing will soon disappear from your speech." But I still say it and say it gladly. There's something honourable about having a wife, particularly when you have a good wife.

Marriage also brings favour. The Bible says in Proverbs 18:22 *Amp*, "he who finds a wife finds a good thing and obtains favour from the Lord." You see, God looks favourably on marriage, especially on marriages that are entered into and built biblically. The Bible also says that after God had made Adam and Eve, He looked at all He had done and said it was very good. Other things He said were good, but when He made and saw both of them He called it "very good." So there's something about marriage that brings you to a place where God says this is very good. Marriage is a good thing, if it is done well.

God also gives married couples the pleasure of sex. Many don't understand that sex is a joy designed to be exclusive to marriage. The permanence and commitment of marriage makes sex safe (no fear of sexually transmitted diseases) and purposeful (aiding oneness). Statistics make it clear that contrary to what the glossy magazines would have you believe, married couples have sex more often than single people and have better quality sex than single people.

Marriage is also about companionship. It's wonderful to have one person to journey through life with; that special someone who's got your back no matter what. This is the one person who is praying for you, rooting for you, working with and walking with you. One of the things I enjoy most is lying next to my wife at the end of the day holding each other as we watch TV, laughing at something we remember or just enjoying being with each other. It's great to always have someone to share good news or bad news with; to talk about and plan the future with. It's great!

An important thing to note however is all these things must be nurtured. They don't come automatically as in fairy tales. A marriage can bring dishonour and favour; and marriage and companionship can be lacking. The key to enjoying these blessings of marriage is actively nurturing and cultivating them. If these things are not carefully nurtured and cultivated in marriage, they can quickly fly out of the window. So will marriage make you happy? I leave that to you to decide at the end of this chapter.

So who is marriage for?

To enjoy the honour, favour, pleasure, and companionship of marriage; the individuals within the marriage must have wisdom and be mature and responsible. Marriage is not for kids; it's not just about fitting into the glass shoe. You need to come to a certain point in your life where you assess yourself and ask, "Do I really have what it takes to sustain a marriage?" You don't get married just because you want to. You must be able to say "I am ready enough now to give to somebody sacrificially for a lifetime."

Marriage is not for wimps. It is not for people who will chicken out when things get tough. Marriage is also not for the faint-hearted. Nor is it a 100 metre dash, it is a marathon. A pastor friend of mine always says this: "Sola, it's a 'loooong' race." So you must build up your stamina. You can't afford to complain when you've only done 12 years; brace yourself and strengthen your limbs because it's a looong race.

DON'T PICK OR EAT THE FRUIT BEFORE IT BECOMES RIPE

Anytime you hear the word maturity, what comes to mind? For me, one of the words that come to mind is fruit, because when a tree comes to maturity, you have the fruit of the tree. Now think about this: Maturity means to come into fullness. A tree bears fruit when it is so full of sap that it has to send the sap through the branches, through the stem, down to a place where it releases something that is nice, juicy, flavoured and colourful; not for itself, but for somebody else. Do you get the point? The fruit of a tree is the only thing that the tree does not really need. No tree really survives on its fruits; it's there for the enjoyment of other people.

"*.A tree bears fruit when it is so full of sap that it has to send the sap through the branches, through the stem, down to a place where it releases something that is nice, juicy, flavoured and colourful, not for itself, but for somebody else.*"

Marriage should only happen when you have fruits ripe enough to give; when you come to a point in your life when you are so full of sap, so full of God, so full of goodness that you have something to share with somebody else. Even if they take it away from you, you are not left deficient. You see, the problem with people is that they don't even have enough fruit for themselves. So when they get married, they often ask "what is left is for me?"

Marriage is not just for mature people, it's also for responsible people. It's for people who are full and are ready to share or give. Being responsible is that you have it and you also give it. Let me explain to you what the difference is. 1 Corinthians 13:11 *NKJV* says; "When I was a child, I spoke as a child; I thought as a child, I understood as a child, but when I became a man, I put away childish things."

One of the signs of childishness is selfishness. I love my kids greatly, and they often tell me, "Dad please take us to MacDonald's, I want chicken nuggets and fries." So I go to McDonalds and get them their hearts desire, I buy the nuggets, the fries, the drinks and the ice cream. Once in a while I ask for just one of the fries, and they say "Daddy, this is mine, please buy some for yourself" - they are not mature. They have it but they are not willing to give it. What they have, they want to keep for themselves. They are not willing to extend what they have to be a blessing to someone else.

7 POINTS TO CONSIDER BEFORE YOU GET MARRIED

These points will help you to determine if you and your intended are ready for marriage.

1. ARE YOU PHYSICALLY MATURE?

It is impossible for an eight year-old girl to get married. This happens in some cultures, but it is really abuse because she has not yet developed what is called the secondary sexual characteristics. Her body is not yet mature. When a girl reaches puberty, usually around 13, her body begins to produce eggs and she begins to develop physical features that indicate maturity. Even so she has a way to go and it is only around, 18 years of age that is fully formed and physically matured. Some girls as young as 15 desire to be married but are they physically mature? I would say no. Even the 18 year old who is physically mature, may not yet be responsible enough for marriage.

2. ARE YOU PSYCHOLOGICALLY MATURE?

Some people ask what age you should get married. That is a complex question to answer because you could have a 43 year-old man who behaves like a 13 year-old boy. You could also have a 24 year-old boy who behaves like a 45 year-old man. So what is more important is 'psychological maturity'. Physical age is a good indicator but it is not enough. Statistics have shown that those who got married between the ages of 20 and 22 were twice as likely to divorce as those who got married between the ages of 24-26 and above- ref

There's a point in your life when one becomes mature, and it is not indicated by age. It is something that other people realise because they see it in ones speech, behaviour and level of understanding.

"Some people ask what age you should get married. That is a complex question to answer because you could have a 43 year-old man who behaves like a 13 year-old boy. You could also have a 24 year-old boy who behaves like a 45 year-old man."

A prayer that is prayed for young men where I come from says, "May you not marry your girlfriend and think she's your wife; and may you not meet your wife and call her a girlfriend." That's a good prayer to pray. It is spiritual blindness for you to see 'wife material' and marry 'girlfriend material.' A lot of men are in pain now because they married a 'girlfriend' not a 'wife.' A lot of women are suffering now because they married a 'boyfriend' and not a 'husband.' It takes a spiritually mature and responsible person to have their eyes open to see a wife or a husband.

ARE YOU GIRLFRIEND OR WIFE MATERIAL?

Eleazar was a man who understood this well. When Abraham sent him to get a wife for Isaac, the condition he gave was, 'whoever I ask her for water, and she goes to get water for me and (as an extra) also gets water for my animals' (see Genesis 24). He was looking out for the person who would be ready to go the extra mile and help. Water was very integral in the domestic life of the Palestinians. He knew she would literally spend her life around the well, washing, cooking and the likes. While I am not saying that the woman needs to be tied to the sink to be a wife, one of the major needs of a man is domestic support. Eleazar was not interested in the ear rings, neck rings and frankincense which adorned the women nor did the look for a woman who knew how to swing her waist as she walked!

A lot of men look at the externals (dressing, comportment); some even look out for signs of spirituality such as praying long or knowing many scriptures. Marrying someone who is high stepping or spiritual is good but as the Bible says, a wife is basically a 'helpmeet'. You don't look and just say, "I like her combination, red on red…hmm…colour coded" or, "I like a man who dresses like that." Rather one should ask 'Can she look after a home?' 'Can he lead a family?' and 'Will he read bedtime stories to our children?'. Those are some of the more important things that keep marriages going, not the colour coding.

WHAT DOES A GOOD WIFE LOOK LIKE?

Recently, my wife began to teach single women about what it means to be a wife. The Bible says the older women should teach the younger women how to love their husbands and children- Titus 2:4. I would have thought that love would come naturally for women but the scripture they have to be taught to love their husbands properly and to be home makers. That means what we may think is love (holding hands and walking on the beach) is not the kind of love that will make a marriage or home hold together. No matter how sophisticated a man is, he wants a wife and a homemaker. A lot of married men are still waiting for the wife to emerge from the woman they married. That may be why some men are not experiencing favour in their businesses and in their lives. When their woman become's a wife, they'll have a new experience because a wife is a dream maker and not a dream breaker. A wife is supportive and helps to make things happen for her husband.

"No matter how sophisticated a man is, he wants a wife. A lot of married men are still waiting for their wives to emerge. That's why they are not experiencing favour in their businesses and in their lives. When their women become wives, they'll see a new experience because a wife is a dream maker and not a dream breaker"

ARE YOU A BOYFRIEND OR HUSBAND MATERIAL?

The Bible says that "for this reason a man shall leave his father and mother and be joined to his wife" (Mark 10:7 *NKJV*). That is what makes a husband: *one that leaves*. That's the difference between physical maturity and psychological maturity. A husband is a man that does not keep saying, 'My parents did it like this…' I say 'Grow up!' Paul wrote, 'When I was a child, I spoke as a child…' it's important to leave childish things behind.

A real husband is one that has left home; not one that still goes back home to ask for advice: "So mummy how do we do it? Which house should we pick? Which job should I accept? Which school should the children go to?" Men who still need monitoring by parents are not husbands; they are just boys. And a husband is a man who is ready to head a home – to protect, provide for and lead his family.

Some young women tend to look for guys with a good dress sense; one who has a house, a car, and money - the man who is the talk of the town and whom all the ladies like (like LL Cool J which stands for L(adies) L(ove) Cool J)! These are the same things that actually begin to cause problems after marriage. The ladies still flock around him and the wife has to fight them off (sometimes literally). Instead such ladies are advised when looking for a husband, to look for somebody who is financially responsible and generous, somebody who loves children, who is caring and gentle and somebody who is emotionally mature and responsible.

3. ARE YOU EMOTIONALLY MATURE?

Emotional maturity and responsibility is being full of something and having enough to give. Let me give you this example.

"A lot of young women tend to look for a guy with a nice sense of dressing; one who has a house, a car, and money. they like a man who is the talk of the town. the same things they like are the things that actually begin to cause problems after marriage."

I have a car and I like my car a lot, but I have a bad habit that relates to it. I take risks in the sense that I tend not to fill up until I am on reserve. Even when my reserve lights come on I drive on, seeing how long I can push it till filling up is imperative. I wonder 'Can I get to church?', sometime I even crazily start speaking in tongues to 'add more fuel' (God have mercy)! . Recently, I had just broken through the motorway when the car began to stall. I called my wife, hoping she had a full tank, but her tank was also on reserve (talk about living on the edge), so she could not come out to help me. Eventually, I had to call a car rescue company, wait for about 45 minutes in the cold, and be towed to the petrol station.

> "That's how marriage is. A lot of people get married on reserve tank - just enough to keep moving so that the other person will think they are headed somewhere. You think, 'Once this person comes, he will keep filling my tank for me'. What you don't know is that the guy himself is on reserve, his engine is about to fail,"

That's how some marriage are. A lot of people get married on a reserve tank emotionally – they have just enough self esteem and self love to keep moving so that the other person will think they are headed somewhere. They think, 'Once this person comes, he will keep filling my tank for me'. What they don't know is that the guy himself is on reserve, his engine is about to fail, his brakes are gone, and he's just waiting for a ride. He is saying, 'She has a car, she has a house, and she has this and that; and she's marrying me, I must be something special. I'll just manoeuvre and we will ride together'. So people make their vows on reserve, get married on reserve, go on honeymoon on reserve, and use up all their fuel quickly.

Once they are back home and the real business of marriage begins, they try to start the car and when it does not respond, the arguments begins, "You mean you did not come with a full tank?" they say to each other. They are trying to draw on each other emotionally, and no one has anything to give. These types of couple are in real trouble.

Some fare better in that one party comes with half a tank while the other is full. The full tanker is happy to fill up what's lacking in the half tanker for a while; but soon gets tired of the extra baggage. Oftentimes, he or she cuts loose and says "I'm off."

Many married people are battling with low self-esteem issues, serious insecurity and hoping their spouse will sort them out. Do you know how challenging it is to carry somebody that you always have to pump up all the time? A lot of women are married to men who are not sure of themselves. They ask "Am I okay? Did I do well in that?" She has to spend all her time pumping up and encouraging the man. Some of us are so damaged that we are leaky that we cant even retain what is poured in us; every assurance and complaint given to us leaks right out because there isn't enough self worth to believe and receive it.

So, will marriage make you happy? Only if you have a full tank or a very mature and patient spouse who is a full tanker! You should get married only when you are strong enough to build other people up when they are down. Before I got married, I had to get to a point where I realised I had more than enough in me to stick with it and also to give to that person to pull them up. If you know you have emotional wounds or issues - take time to attend to them before you get married - it will help you and your future spouse.

4. Are You Financially Mature?

Marriage is for people who are financially mature and responsible. What does that mean?

It means that you must be financially full – and that is relative. It does not mean being able to buy a big house or having a particular kind of car. It means spending according to ones earning power. Driving a Porsche or a Jeep and the likes is not inappropriate if someone can afford it; but if a man can only afford to run a car that has a 1.3 litre tank and he buys a gas guzzling jeep, he is financially immature. If he then hooks up with a woman who has a 4.3 litre approach to life when he can only afford a 1.3litre tank, he is very foolish. She will be dissatisfied and he will be bankrupt! it does not require much to be filled; but if he buys a guzzler he will need more financial fullness.

You know you are financially immature if you're always in debt. It shows you are porous. But if a person is financially mature, they have enough for themselves and to give. I encourage young women to ask those who want to marry them for their tithing record. If he's stingy towards God, what do you think he'll be to you? Look at how much he gives when he gives offerings. Observe how he responds to other people in need. It doesn't matter whether he drives a Lexus jeep - if he is stingy by nature, what you'll have on your hands is a major liability and not an asset.

Being financially mature means being a good manager of the resources you have and being content with what you have on the way to where you want to be. 1 Timothy 6:6 *NKJV* says "Now godliness with contentment is great gain". Living within ones means and with an eye to the future is the mark of the financially mature person.

5. Are You Socially Mature?

The person who is socially mature is one who
- can manage their response and is not entirely driven by their emotions or feelings
- knows the appropriate response in a variety of situations
- can relate with a variety of people
- is accommodating and hospitable.

A successful marriage is also dependent on having the social skills to relate with each other and significant others well. Many marriages break up because one or both spouses do not know how to manage and interact socially with other key people – be it a boss, a mother in-law or a bank manager. Some promotions at work are lost because a spouse's behaviour at the office party discredits the other spouse and many family and in-law relationships are strained because one spouse didn't bite their tongue. We must learn which battles to fight and which ones to concede.

A socially mature person is able to relate with others with respect, courtesy and consideration.

6. Are You Sexually Mature?

A person who is ready for marriage is somebody who is sexually mature and responsible.

Somebody who is sexually mature and responsible is comfortable with themselves as a sexual being. Such a person knows that his or her sexuality is a God given gift and that it is good to give expression to it within marriage. Such a person is not shy or hung up about sex. A sexually mature person knows that God designed sex to be about giving to another person and sharing a sacred act. Some one who is struggling with masturbation or pornography is not sexually mature; because this indicates a self-focused and self-gratifying attitude to sex which is not godly.

Also somebody who is sexually matured is able to be content with one person sexually. A man or woman with a roving eye or who is flirtatious is indicating that they are not a 'one man' or 'one woman' person. There may be trouble ahead. A sexually mature person can keep his zipper up (or her legs crossed); he or she is disciplined.

"He also has to be somebody who is sexually disciplined, which means he knows how to keep his zipper up. He is not somebody who is always flirting with other people."

Thirdly, somebody who is sexually responsible is able to make themselves sexually available within marriage and won't use sex as a bargaining tool. A friend who was struggling with his sex life confided in me saying "I'm not a wicked man. My wife works so hard all day, and when she's home she takes care of children, cooks the food, and looks after the home. She is also very active in church. I feel so bad asking her for sex after all that". Nevertheless his wife insists "You can wake me up anytime, I'm your wife." Now between you and I, is that a fair place to be? No, but life puts us there sometimes. If you have been thinking that marriage will give you sex unlimited you'll find that there is also "limited edition sex." This woman's behaviour demonstrates the kind of sacrifical nature it takes to make marriage work and that what sexual maturity looks like – its not just about one's needs but meeting our spouse's need as well.

7. ARE YOU SPIRITUALLY MATURE?

Lastly, only those who are spiritually mature should get married. Spiritual maturity will touch every aspect of your life and should be your first consideration. I'm ending this chapter to let you know that if you are not yet there, you need to be. Spiritual maturity is being spiritually full.

Being spiritually full isn't about speaking in tongues but being filled with the Holy Spirit. It means having the fruit of the Spirit evident in your life. According to Galatians 5:22, "the fruit of the spirit is Love, Joy, Peace, Faithfulness, Long suffering, Self control, Goodness, Kindness, and Gentleness." If these things are evident in your life you will be content and you won't need anyone to make you happy because you carry your own happiness with you - your own love, joy and peace. You are full and have enough to give.

Your wife might not be giving you any love or your husband could be giving you stress or strife at home, but if you're full of the love of God, you can manage better. Your spouse might be a cantankerous person, like dripping water from a roof, but the peace of God which passes all understanding is able to guard your heart and mind. Regardless of the pressures of life, if you have the Holy Spirit at work powerfully in your life- you can keep going.

The presence of the fruit of the Spirit in your life also enables you to extend yourself to others – to be loving and kind and to make choices that honour others. The Holy Spirit can help you to remain faithful to your spouse through challenging times. Self-control which the Holy Spirit gives, helps you to manage lust, even when you're spouse isn't sexually available to you. Faithfulness keeps you from having an affair. The Holy Spirit can also enable you to be patient and longsuffering when you're irritable and want to blow your fuse; somehow you have grace to bear it a little while longer.

So, back to our original question at the beginning of this chapter -will marriage make you happy? From my experience, I think the answer is 'No it won't, if you cannot say yes to many of the seven questions we have considered in this chapter'; and most especially if you do not have the Holy Spirit and His fruit manifesting in you. But all is not lost, there is hope. The point is to find out where you are deficient and begin to prayerfully ask God to grow you in those areas.

CHAPTER 3

ARE YOU A GUEST AT YOUR OWN WEDDING?

So many wonder what I mean by being a guest at your own wedding. The host of an event should be relaxed and in charge, it's the invited guests that are sometimes nervous because they may not know the other people at the wedding or what's on the agenda. From that perspective it just doesn't make sense that you can be a guest at your own wedding. Well I'll tell you a real story, my story. I felt like a guest at my own wedding because as the day approached the reality of what lay ahead began to dawn on me. I was a young bachelor, making just about enough to tick over, I shared a flat with another single man and couldn't cook. I was in debt due to a student loan and apart from pastoring a church and attending bible school, I was also running a small business on the side. This was hardly an auspicious start, bearing in mind that my wife was coming from a well to do family. It suddenly hit me that I was taking on responsibility for another human being, I thought to myself; 'I am barely providing for myself, how will I provide for another person as well?' The future looked uncertain.

WILL YOU FAST ON YOUR WEDDING DAY?

Such was my trepidation that by the wedding day the tension was visible. While everyone was excited I was like a stranger at my own wedding. While people were talking about the car, the ribbons, the cake, I thought to myself, 'who is really getting married here?' During the reception, my father-in-law leaned over and asked me why I was not eating. My reply was, "I am fasting." It was the truth. I had to fast because I didn't know what the future held and I needed God to come through! During the exchange of vows, I felt like I was having an out-of-body experience when I said "I do." In my mind, I actually said, "Do you?" I felt like an observer. It was not until the following day it really dawned on me that I was married!

DO YOU KNOW YOUR FUTURE SPOUSE?

Whilst my trepidations were due to realisation of the financial implications of being married; many people are guests at their own weddings because they don't really know the person they are getting married to. They may have suspicions that cause them anxiety and as a result they cant really relax and enjoy the event. Others are guests at their own weddings because they haven't even discovered who they are themselves. So, they think they are Jane Smith, but they are really Jane Shabadabadoo; and if they did know who they were, they probably wouldn't be hooking up with this person.

"Many people are guests at their own weddings because they don't know who they are really getting married to. They feel they know but they really don't know."

PEOPLE PLAN FOR THEIR WEDDING INSTEAD OF THEIR MARRIAGE

A lot of people, especially ladies, are guests at their own weddings because they are preoccupied with the preparations towards the day. The flowers must be fuchsia, the cake must be have this kind of icing and the decorations must be imported from Paris. Some people have pre-planned their marriage before meeting the spouse; before the man came they matched his tie with the colour of the cake. They have given little thought to the nature of the vows they are taking, their readiness to make them and the sort of person who can honour those vows. Marriage is a very important and crucial decision in a person's life. It is a solemn institution that is sacred to God. It was instituted by God and anybody entering into it must enter it soberly and not casually, having weighed the implications.

ASK "DO I?" BEFORE YOU SAY, "I DO!"

Before you say "I do", make sure you ask "Do I?', if you plan to enjoy your marriage. These are two different questions. One is a question while the other is a commitment.

"Do I?" means, its important to ask 'do I want to spend the rest of my life with this woman?' Do I want to spend the rest of my life with this man? Do I want this man to be the father of my children? Do I want my children to look like this man? Do I want my children to behave like this man? Do I want my children to look like this woman that I'm barely enduring now? Will my future wife end up looking or behaving like her mother (and am I ok with that)? Is this the face I want to see last thing at night and first thing in the morning? You need to consider all this before you say "I do".

"Make sure you ask "Do I?" before you say "I do" if you plan to enjoy your marriage. These are two very different things. One is a question while the other is a commitment."

Marriage is always enjoyable when you know who you are getting married to and accept them for who they really are. The key word here is acceptance. I feel a buzz when two people who I think are suited hook up. But, I always challenge them to ask the right questions. I'm always trying to get them to consider if they really know the person they want to tie the knot with. The truth of the matter is, you will enjoy your marriage if you know the person and are able to accept them for who they really are. The truth is there is no perfect person; but you should really know an individual before you enter into a marriage with them so that you can appreciate what you are getting into but unfortunately many people really don't consider all the facts.

"Marriage is always enjoyable when you know who you are getting married to and accept them for who they really are. The key word here is acceptance."

THE LITTLE THINGS THAT CAUSE BIG PROBLEMS IN A MARRIAGE

So what then are the things that cause problems in a marriage? I've put them down to four key things. These include the following:

1. Being ill-prepared for the marriage journey.
2. Not asking the right questions before the wedding
3. Having and holding onto unrealistic expectations.
4. Not keeping your vows.

These are essentially the four main things that lead to a bad marriage. In the last chapter we addressed the first of these topics. In section two we will talk about the third and fourth topic at length. The rest of this chapter is devoted at looking at the second topic.

Many people marry a virtual stranger. They do not invest enough time in really getting to know a person and thus often find interesting surprises on the other side of the wedding ceremony.

This section should help married people who are having challenges to diagnose the reasons for marital problems. For those that are unmarried, this is a checklist of important things to know about a fiancée that will help you go into marriage with a good knowledge of each other.

12 THINGS YOU SHOULD KNOW ABOUT YOUR SPOUSE BEFORE YOU GET MARRIED

1. IDENTITY of your future spouse

Do you know your partner's name? This is no joke at all. You think he's John Smith, but he is actually Peter Doe. I have known people marry people without knowing their real names. Some people have changed their names due to fraudulent activity and have acquired a identity with the new name (sometimes omitting to tell their future spouse their previous name and character). We once had two single ladies in our church dating the same guy (he had presented a slightly different name to each one so it took a while to figure out they were dating the same person). It is not extreme to urge you to make sure that the person you are marrying is who they say they are - check their passport and check their record.

2. STATUS

Is the person you desire single or married? Crazy as it may seem, one lady told my wife of her discovery on getting married that her husband was already married. His wife lived in another country, a fact he had omitted to tell the lady who spoke with my wife. She was heartbroken when my wife told her that she was not married legally because the man she thought she married was already married and so could not be her husband! Please don't be a guest at your own wedding. You may think you are marrying a single person, but please do take the time to find out enough to be really sure you are.

3. GENDER

Are you marrying a man or a woman? The wonders of medicine mean that people can change their sex, and people have dated someone they initially thought was a woman only to find out 'she' used to be a man. Strange but true! More common however is the trend of closet homosexuals parading as heterosexuals. I have known of several women who have married men who are gay or bi-sexual; so when I encourage you to consider the gender issue, I am also talking about their sexual preference and propensity. If there are rumours about someone you are dating having same sex inclinations- do yourself a favour, hit it on the head and ask them about it. You don't want the pain of a marriage to someone who is neither attracted to you nor anyone of your gender!

4. FAMILY AND FRIENDS

It is important to know that when you marry, you don't just marry the person alone - you marry their entire family. Did you know that there are so many people attached to that person you love so much – they come with the package (buy 1 get 20 free)! Because these people will be a part of your life, its important to get to know your intended's family. How do they do things as a family – what are their attitudes to money or parenting and how do they resolve conflict for example? Its' likely your intended's inherited those traits. It's also important to know the friends of the person you are getting married to. Do you like his or her friends; also what do your intended's friends say about the type of person she is? My wife always tells me that one of the things that recommended me to her was my friends - they were mature and spiritual and responsible people - it spoke well of me. You know what they say friends of a feather flock together. It's also important that your intended like and is able to relate with your friends. Why? You'll find out when you get married that the lines blur and your friendships will often be enjoyed as a couple. Many of them will stop being 'your' friend or 'my' friend and become 'our' friend.

5. Beliefs

Does this person have the same beliefs as you? You may think you are marrying a Christian, but you might not be. I know somebody who got married to a man; on the morning following the wedding he woke up and rolled his Muslim prayer mat out and started saying Muslim prayers. The lady asked, "What are you doing?" And he said, "I'm praying to my God." It turned out that he had pretended to be a Christian in order to get married to her; once the mission was accomplished, he could revert to his true self and beliefs. Don't look at what the person calls themselves, if a person is really a Christian, it will show in their values, speech, thoughts and actions.

6. History

You need to know the person's history. Its important to know about your intended's social, educational, spiritual, relational, family (and anything else you can think of) history. I know a lady who had a rather racy past, she had slept with a lot of men, was into nudist camps and all sorts. She wanted to know if she should tell her intended. Her pastors advice was 'yes, at the right time'. Would you want full disclosure? I personally think it's important to disclose all, because if you don't disclose everything, the person is a guest at their own wedding; they don't really know who they are saying "I do" to. There is a possibility that whatever is in your history will show up again and if they knew who you really are they may say 'I don't'. Better rejection before than after the wedding I say. True love means accepting the person as they really are. If they can't accept your past, they can't handle you.

7. CREDIT

It is helpful to know the credit history of your intended spouse. You do not want to discover after the wedding that your spouse owes all the banks in town! The fact that a guy drives an M-class Mercedes Benz doesn't mean he's doing well - it may really be owned by Barclaycard. If you marry him you inherit his credit history, good or bad. Its important to know what financial liabilities you are starting married life with and to have a plan to be free of it.

8. WEAKNESSES

It is easy to list all the things that you like in a person when you are in love and want to get married. However, people seldom ask themselves: "What don't I like in my intended partner?" It is better to ask the questions now and avoid rude awakenings in the future. Gary Chapman in his book Love Languages told of a lady who was raving about her fiancée. Her mother gently cautioned her saying ' Darling, are you aware he's been in a mental institution for 5 years?'. 'Oh mum', the lady replied ' he's been out for 3 whole months'. How's that for self delusion! That young lady was not facing up to the fact that she was hooking up with some one who would likely be struggling with psychiatric issues for sometime and perhaps a lifetime. Have you looked your fiancée's weakness's squarely in the face and asked, can I live with this for a lifetime?

9. BAGGAGE

What kind of baggage has this person come with? What personal or emotional issues are going to impact your marriage? Are there emotional traumas from family, childhood or teenage incidents (such as rape or abuse) or guilt from having an abortion; is there a soul tie from a previous relationship or a parental divorce that has had deep effects? You may also want to look into family of origin issues – traits and patterns. Are there any curses in this person's family? If you don't believe in curses, just study the Kennedy family. It is important to find out what spiritual things your intended has inherited and you need to assess if you are if you are ready to fight the battles involved.

10. MOTIVES

It is also important to ask 'what is this person's motive for getting married?' So many singles make a permanent decision on temporary circumstances. They rush into marriage because they are lonely; want to get out of their parents' house or in order to escape being 'the last one on the shelf' amongst their friends. They want to prove to their friends that they can marry and have a "Mrs." or 'Mr.' in front of their name. Marriage is easy to get into and hard to get out of - make sure your fiancée is going in with the right motives.

11. THE FUTURE

What is this individuals aspirations and plans for the future and how will that impact the marriage? My wife and I have been watching an American TV series in which one of the couples marriage is strained because the husband's ambition and drive is putting his family in second place; which in turn is causing resentment and withdrawal in the wife. So ask yourself, what will we be like in five years, in ten and in twenty? Will we work together or will our aspirations and desires drive us apart. And perhaps more importantly, if a choice needs to be made, will my spouse choose our family or his goals?

12. YOUR DECISION

After asking all these questions, you should now ask yourself, "Do I really want to be married to this person?" Once you are married, all these issues will stare you in the face. Love, people say, is blind, but marriage is an eye-opener. The things you didn't see before you got married will become clear afterwards.

Take the time to get to know your spouse before marriage – you will be glad you did on the other side.

PART TWO

THE PROBLEMS IN MARRIAGE

EXPOSING AND EXPELLING THE BAD THINGS THAT DESTROY MARRIAGES

CHAPTER FOUR

THE BATTLE FOR YOUR MARRIAGE

FIGHT FOR YOUR MARRIAGE

One of the reasons why good marriages go bad is because there are some elements seeking to destroy marriages. We are at war and there are enemies all around. Many times you don't see them but a whole army is often arrayed against a marriage. It is important to know your enemy and get acquainted with his tools, his devices and strategies.

Who are we fighting? What are the entities we are wrestling with in our marriage? Let's give them categories. They have ranks and they come in at different times or seasons of a marriage. I have named them below.

THE MARRIAGE KILLERS

- **Militants**
- **Intruders**
- **Undercover agents**
- **Hired Assassins**
- **Terrorist network**

We have **militants**, who come to harass you. They come, charge and they retreat again. They kidnap and then hold out for a ransom. The **intruders** come in to steal time, energy & money. There are also **undercover agents** like the CIA, KGB of the marriage. They come in and operate covertly. They come as plainclothes people from the other side so you don't know them when they come and mingle in your marriage. Then you have the **hired assassins**. And then you have a **Terrorist network** like Al Qaeda. These are the master planners, the orchestrators of the damage to your marriage. They are not seen. Like Osama Bin Laden, you just know he is there but you don't see him. Once in a while he sends you a video threat. This entire team is orchestrated and they have a headquarters which is controlled by the terrorist network.

THE MILITANTS

In modern day society, work is an example of a militant in marriage. The demands of the modern day corporate system can be harsh and unrelenting. People work longer hours (with people in the city having working days that start at 7am and end at 7pm or 8pm), leaving little time for oneself let alone a family. The pay may be good but they get their pound of flesh.

Many people also often take work home in the evenings and over the weekend – so even when they are home there's little time to relate with their spouse. It has been said that couples often spend as little as seven minutes a day having uninterrupted focused face to face discussion. It is no wonder couples are drifting apart.

HELP! A CHILD JUST CRAWLED INTO MY BED!

Another example of 'militants' are your children. Paul admonishes us in 1 Corinthians Chapter 7 by saying, "*If a single person marries she has not sinned but those who marry **will face many troubles in this life** and I want to spare you …*" Even though children are a blessing, let me say they can be troublesome! Before children came it was just the two of you; once a child comes in your attention can no longer be on just the two of you- your attention is divided from now on. Children often mean sleepless nights, increased responsibility, financial demands, lack of appreciation and less sex. It is not surprising that research (ref) shows that when a baby comes into a marriage conflict multiplies eight times. If there was heat in your house before children, get ready for thunderstorms. It is said that by a child's first birthday, most mothers are less happy about their marriages.

Children bring a completely different dynamic to the relationship. I am still recovering from our last child. Till he was two and a half years old, he would visit our room at least three times every night.

He would come on visitation with his blankets saying, "Daddy, I'm afraid" or "Daddy, I'm cold" or "I had a bad dream". His sleep deprived mom was not sympathetic at all towards his antics. You need to cast the darling out of your room because many kids have taken the place of the husband. After a while, just so they can get some sleep, many couples allow their children to sleep in their bed and drive a wedge between them (sometimes one adult retreats to the sitting room to get a good nights sleep, leaving his marital bed to the children!). If this continues unchecked, it eventually becomes a normal part of life, bringing an extinguisher to romance and eventually, your sex life.

THE INTRUDERS

Next are the intruders. This is represented by time-stealing gadgets such as the television, computer or telephone. Many couples will flop in front of the TV for hours each night, giving attention to strangers on the box and not talk to each other. Others still are actively courting other people on social network sites online as their spouse does housework in another room. Intruders are not like the militants. They are rebels. They are not a part of the deal so they creep in slowly and subtly.

Another example of an intruder is financial debt; it can creep up and get a hold of you unawares. We start off with a few indulgences on a store card, and then we get a hire purchase agreement for a bigger car and a mortgage for a bigger house to accommodate our growing family. Some of us are driven into debt by fantasy aspirations - we want to live the dream in a nice house, in the right postcode and we want our children to attend the best private schools. Before we know it, we have accrued debt that hangs on our neck like an albatross. You do the sums again and again but you realise you don't make enough to honour the loans. Now problems are compounded, not only can you not pay the loan, your spouse is angry with you because of that!

Sometimes prevailing economic conditions can intrude on a marriage. An economic meltdown or credit crunch may mean people cannot be choosey with where they work and one partner ends up moving to another city or country to work. As a result the husband and wife may only see each other at weekends, once a month or only every few months. The separation can strain a marriage, leaving the parent with the children feeling like a single parent and the one away from home lonely and estranged.

Still other couples struggle with illnesses or medical conditions such as infertility. Also as couples age, hitting their mid 40's or 50's their bodies can become less agile; and lack of proper care in diet and exercise can result in medical complications. A woman in her mid 20's can have a habit of eating late and going to bed shortly after meals; due to high metabolism she may not gain weight. However as such a person hits her 40's she can't get away with this. That's why some women who started life as a size 8 can become a size 18 after 20 years of marriage – of course the excess weight puts stress on their organs, cause back problems and such. Of course, these issues affect feelings of vitality and well being which impact marital life.

Last but not least, many marriages are under pressure because of the intrusion of in-laws. When not properly managed, interaction with each others family can be a point of much contention. Sometimes key people are not willing to accept the boundaries that the marriage of a son or daughter entails. Some mothers are unwilling to give up their position of influence upon their son, and some fathers wish to continue to protect their daughter. Sometimes its brothers or sisters that want to continue to claim the time and ears of their brother and sister who is now married. These vying claims can cause a lot of problems in marriage.

THE UNDERCOVER AGENTS

Undercover agents as the word implies operate under cover; undercover is anything that does not show on the radar. The greatest wars have not been won by sending 2000 foot men or a battalion of army; many are won by strategy. Sometimes all that is needed is one spy - somebody that looks like a friend and nobody knows has a dangerous agenda. The Trojan War in Greece was won by undercover tactics. The city was fortified and its inhabitants thought it could never be penetrated. Their enemies however had a plan. They built a large wooden horse and gave it to the inhabitants of the city as a gift for their king. In the daytime they celebrated the receipt of the gift; but at night as the city slept, the enemies hidden within the horse made their way out, crept into the homes of the soldiers and the leaders within the city and killed them.

In the same way, undercover agents enter into your home and your heart stealthily, and they often come as a result of the intruders. Anger can easily arise from the frustration of mounting bills and debt or the intrusion of in-laws. You may hear something like, "You spent it all, I gave you the credit card and you just went and irresponsibly spent it to the limit" or "Your nosy mum is really getting on my nerves!" Anger and un-forgiveness can so easily creep in. These emotions can creep up on us unaware but they are deadly.

When my wife teaches on conflict resolution, she instructs that some of us are like rhinos while others are hedgehogs. 'Rhinos' readily display their anger but hedgehogs recoil and withdraw. Hedgehogs internalise their anger and it becomes resentment. You know what resentment is? It's stewed anger. It seems to be over but fifteen years later, he or she says "Yes! That's what you did to me in 1967!" The most dangerous types of marital strife are when the couple are frustrated and dissatisfied but don't talk about it. Many just keep swallowing the pain and taking all the junk without discussing and trying to resolve it– until a day when one person decides they have had enough. T.D. Jakes talks of the man who tells his wife he's taking out the garbage and never returns. She can't figure out what's wrong because he never said anything and she thought things were hunky dory between them; but they couldn't have been, he just chose not to talk about it and one day he decided he couldn't take it anymore and left! This is how the little annoying things pile up and cause big damage to a marriage.

"The most dangerous types of marital strife are the ones in which couples are frustrated and dissatisfied but don't talk about it. They just keep swallowing the pain and taking all the junk without saying anything"

Resentment is a serious thing. That's why the Bible says in Ephesians 4:26 *NKJV*, "*… do not let the sun go down on your wrath*". The scripture enjoins us to "be angry but sin not!" In the Bible says anger rests in the bosom of fools which means if you let anger rest in your heart, it will cause destruction. When you let anger settle it grows and can become a monster. Resentment can build to the point where one begins to take it out on the children, the spouse and other people.

"You see, the greatest wars have not been won by sending 2000 foot men or a battalion of army. All that is needed is one spy - somebody that looks like a friend and nobody knew he had a dangerous agenda."

Un-forgiveness, envy and jealousy are some of the other destructive undercover elements. Jealousy can be poisonous - the pressure of being constantly monitored can strain a marriage. A jealous spouse will often ask "Where did you go? I saw somebody talking to you. Is he your boyfriend?" These propensities have their root in a poor self-image, past hurts or unmet needs. Left unchecked jealousy can break a marriage. I remember a scene in the movie 'The Aviator' who had his girlfriend's telephone tapped so that he could monitor all her conversations. This kind of action goes to show how extreme and obsessive jealously can become. When she found out she ended the relationship.

"Stop to think before you sleep. Ask yourself that "Am I still angry?" When you let it settle it grows and can later become a monster. Resentment can build to the point that you begin to take it out on your children, your spouse and other people. "

THE HIRED ASSASSINS

The next group are the hired assassins. They are only employed once anger has opened the door and taken full ground. The Bible says we should not give a foothold to the devil. When you open the door to anger it puts its foot in the door and gains access to wreak havoc.

God asked Cain, 'why are you angry? This Bible story centred around two brothers who each gave an offering to God. God preferred Abel's offering and this caused Cain to be angry. In truth the root of his anger was envy; eventually it turned into anger and anger led to murder. Anger is a key that can opens door to evil happenings. Anger can open the door to physical abuse in marriage, to rape in marriage, and even to adultery (perhaps as an act of vengeance for a wrong suffered). I remember speaking with one woman who was hell-bent on getting involved with another man, any man, to pay back her husband for his adulterous affair. I warned her against this because I knew her vengeance could cost her dear. Her act of vengeance could have left her with a sexually transmitted disease, an unwanted illegitimate pregnancy or a divorce.

God had warned Cain when he was just angry but the demon of murder was already lurking at his door; and when he didn't manage anger, anger took control of him. Do you know how generational curses and patterns hit people who are Christians? It is by the doors they open. If you open a door through anger or envy, they can enter. In some families, the generational sin or pattern such as divorce or adultery hits a descendant skips one person who holds fast to God and then goes to a person in the next generation who opens a door. If you rule over your anger you won't open the door to the other deadly sins which follow it.

When deep emotions are not aired and dealt with as they arise in marriage, it can also lead to addictive behaviour. Sometimes people turn to alcohol or drugs or pornography as a way of release or relief.

This brings to mind the account of the fall in Genesis 3:1 *NKJV*. *"Now the serpent was more cunning than any beast of the field which the Lord God had made and he said to the woman has God indeed said you shall not eat of every tree of the garden?"* The serpent did not come until Adam was away. Satan crept in when there was a distance between Adam and Eve. When a union is strong and there is no disconnection between the couples its hard for something destructive to come in. But once there's distance and one or both of the couple spouse is not spiritually alert and Spirit led, they can become open to elements that will pull them further apart.

THE TERRORIST NETWORK

The last group is the terrorist network. It is important for you to know that marriages also face spiritual attack. The bible says God hates divorce, which means Satan loves divorce, because he is the opposite of everything that God is. Just as God desires strong monogamous and joyful marriages and makes His Spirit available to help us achieve it, the enemy loves weak adulterous and unhappy marriages and sets his demons at work to achieve that. There is a whole network of demons, generational sins, curses and patterns that the enemy will try to visit on the children of God. Look at your family – what are the marital patterns in your father's life and in your grandfather's life? Did they have happy monogamous marriages or did they experience polygamy, adultery and physical abuse in their relationship history. If the latter is the case, don't be surprised if you begin to experience difficulties in your marriage designed to a point of frustration so that you can do the same thing they did i.e. cheat on your spouse, beat them up or marry someone else.

Some of you may think this sounds far fetched. If so, I refer you to …….which says," We do not wrestle against flesh or blood but against principalities and powers, against the rulers of the darkness of this age". The truth is that some of our marital problems are of our own making but some are the work of evil masterminds who oppose Gods plan for marriage. There is an interesting scripture in 1 Kings 22:21-22. The Bible says God was frustrated with the kings of Israel and he wanted to destroy them. God was wondering how he was going to do this and an evil spirit volunteered. The scripture says 'So one spirit came forward and stood before the Lord and said, "I will entice him". "By what means?" the Lord asked. "I will go out and be a lying spirit in the mouths of his prophets." Can you see how the enemy works to destroy? He does so by sowing lies in people's minds and causing destruction. When a married couple fight, it's these lying spirits who come and whisper in your ear and amplify the negatives. Those voices that whisper "'Never forgive" or "This will never work, you are better off elsewhere" are demonic. You need to shut them up.

If your marriage has been bombarded by intruders, militants, undercover agents, hired assassins,' or the terrorist network- you can still win. The Bible says this in Ephesians 6:11 (*NKJV*) "Put on the whole armour of God that you may be able to stand against the wiles or the strategies of the devil". Part of the armour is spiritual warfare – prayer and fasting; but the armour also involves wisdom. Read on to find out how not to break up with your spouse; make up!

CHAPTER FIVE

THE LITTLE THINGS THAT DESTROY GOOD MARRIAGES

T he other day I once again witnessed the joining of two people in marriage. As the bride came in gloriously arrayed and looking gorgeous, I couldn't help wondering if the smile would still be as broad six years later. I looked at the dapper groom and wondered if he'd be this trim in six year time. I wondered how much life would change them.

What I am trying to say essentially is that married life is not lived at the wedding ceremony and that unfortunately, what starts on a high note and on a good plain can sometimes degenerate. I'm talking about real life. The truth of the matter is that every marriage will face its challenges, even the best of them. No matter how good a marriage is or how God-ordained it is likely that you will have to fight for your marriage. The reason is simple: we face a real enemy and many of us go into marriage unprepared.

If I sound extreme, take a look at some of the statistics below.

All Marriages will go through Storms

It is claimed that one out of every two married men and one out of every three married woman has had a sexual affair-ref. This means that even in your church, for every three women you count, one has been unfaithful to her spouse, and for every two men that walk even though they may still be married through the door one has been unfaithful.

Approximately 40- 50% of every marriage breaks up and ends up in divorce. The surprising thing however is that 95% of the people who get divorced eventually do remarry. One may have thought that when a person divorces, they would be wary of re-marriage. Yet many still remarry and 76% end up divorcing a second time! And of those who remarry after a second divorce, 86% of them get divorced a third time. Of those who remarry the fourth time, guess what percentage of them divorce again? 93%. Old habits die hard it seems.

It is said that the definition of insanity is for a man to keep doing the same thing but expect a different result. For those who remarry to fail so woefully time and again, it makes it clear that it's a lot easier to have a bad marriage than a good one. In this chapter we want to further examine how some of the things we talked about in the previous chapter can work their way into a marriage and cause it to break down.

THE PROCESS TOWARDS DIVORCE IN MARRIAGE

1.   Dream
2.   Disappointment
3.   Discouragement
4.   Distance
5.   Division
6.   Divorce

1. DREAM OF MARRIAGE (LOVE MATES AND BEDMATES)

Spouses start off as **Love mates with hearts aflutter for each other, excited at even the mention of each others names. This stage is dreamlike – the couple love to** look into one another's eyes (appreciating the twinkle in each hers eyes), they go for walks; hold hands and spend time counting the stars.

As courtship progresses and they plan the wedding, the bride to be has dreamt of the honeymoon since she began playing with Barbie dolls. She's envisaged and anticipated how she will be dressed and fantasised about how ecstatic the romance will be.

To aid this fantasy, they have booked into a fantasy hotel (in a room unlike one they will spend most of their marital life in). They drive to this fantasy hotel in a rented limousine (like Cinderella in her golden carriage) and sleep on satin sheets laid on the bed.

I am sure you get the picture - the only way is down after such a high beginning! How many people sleep on satin sheets every day, drive limousines and sleep in rooms filled with freshly plucked roses every day? The reality is very few do. The honeymoon is unreal; and it introduces new couples into marriage in a very unrealistic way.

If they've done it the right way, at the honeymoon they become **bed mates.** What do I mean by Bed mates? Just watch the newly married, they can barely keep their hands off one other, they are so into each other sexually. At this stage the couple enjoy ongoing physical, emotional and spiritual closeness. They pray together, share and carry one another's burdens, and spend much of their free time together. They believe they will always feel the way they do and that they will be together forever and live happily ever after. That's the dream, but then sooner or later reality dawns.

Somebody said "marriage is like getting a phone call at night. After the ring, you wake up." This basically means after a sweet dream you wake up to reality.

2. DISAPPOINTMENT IN MARRIAGE (ROOM MATES)

The next phase or stage in the marriage is what you call the **down-to-earth stage and it is here that disappointment can set in**. This is the reality stage, when the couple get back home. In the dream honeymoon stage and phase, there are no bills to pay. This is where the rubber meets the road and the daily grind of life begins to impinge on the dreamlike state of the marriage.

This is also the phase where the three big issues of life - money, sex, and power - begin to contend with each other. You might have thought that you would have sex daily or till daybreak, but you've been married long enough to know that's just a fantasy! Then there is the issue of roles and contention about the meaning of submission. Who is the leader and who make what decisions? The famous question about the in-laws may also begin to come up as they make their presence felt. Should we outlaw the in-laws or bring them in? Soon 'Aunt Jenny' is banned from your house due to her meddling ways. You begin to wonder, 'What happened to all the love in the air? What happened to all those stars in his or her eyes?'

At this time you also have to deal with what is really in your bank account or not, as the case may be. A few weeks after getting home the pile of bills begin to mount up- gas, electricity, and water bills (and sometimes a note from the bailiffs!). Reality begins to dawn. This is where you begin to see your spouse as he or she really is, warts and all. Now, there's no more looking into each other's eyes. Instead each one starts finding fault with the other and asking "Why did you keep the lights on?" or "Why did you do this or that?"

I remember a sofa that I bought out of excitement believing some money was coming. It was a leather sofa. I got home and announced to my wife, "I bought a new sofa to go with our new home." She asked, 'Do we have the money?' I said confidently, "its coming." The sofa cost £600. The sellers originally said it was £450 but the final calculations came to about £600. The money I was expecting didn't come in; and so I had this sofa which was meant to be a blessing, but became a huge burden. When you are trying to survive as a young family on a small salary £600 is a lot of money. I used to have nightmares of it chasing me around at night! We still have that brown sofa in the house now. It is worn, but I'm not getting rid of it because I paid for it with my flesh and blood!

As time goes on differences become more obvious. Before marriage many couples when asked about differences will say 'We are very much alike. We love the same things.' Or it may be things that attracted them to each other in the first place that bring conflict and contention. Maybe you married your wife because she is meticulous and organised, then she begins to get into your hair because she's too organised. Or perhaps you married your husband because he is creative; and then you find out that Leonardo da Vinci's house was a mess because of his creativity. I was in Chicago for a conference and a gentleman who used to be in my church and was my flat mate for a while came to visit me in my hotel room. He said, "Pastor Sola, so, you're still like this." I asked him what he meant and replied, "So you still have books scattered all over the place." I said, "Well, that's how I come. That's the package." So he said, "How does your wife cope with you?" I said, "Well, she copes now." There was a time when my wife would take all my books and arrange them. Now she just arranges her own side of the bed, my side looks like Mount Kilimanjaro. The problem is, I don't read books sequentially like most people do; I have been known to read about 20 books at the same time, and I want them spread out near me so I can reach them easily as needed. This is the stage where you learn to navigate your spouse's idiosyncrasies and moods.

The discovery of the less than perfect attributes of our spouses can cause disappointment and one person may begin to say, 'This is not what I bargained for. Somebody has traded the goods.'

Comparisons with other people may also begin, perhaps with a past lover. A lady may think, 'he's not as big as my ex' or not as handsome or his voice is not as deep. A man may think, she's not as caring or beautiful or hardworking as my ex, mum or sister. Disappointment creeps in and settles down. Before long such a couple are simply **Room mates, who share a bed but not their bodies with each other.**

3. Discouragement in Marriage (Flat mates)

From disappointment, people can move into a state of discouragement and that is when they may think "I made a mistake in my choice of a spouse." You begin to wonder, "Did I really marry the right person? Shouldn't I have married so and so? Wouldn't he have treated me better"?

At this point, couples may begin to say hurtful things to each other. They feel so disappointed and discouraged that they each may begin to feel that there is nothing that they can do that is pleasing to each other. Every little thing done or said may elicit complaints. Sometimes in frustration someone in this kind of marriage may to their spouse "I wish I never married you." or "My life would be better if I wasn't married to you." An African adage states 'Words are like raw eggs; once you throw them on the floor and they break you can never pick them up again." Hurtful words have that effect; even though an apology may later be proffered, the hurt they have caused runs deep.

As issues and hurts pile up one partner may, in anger, decide to sleep with his or her back to their spouse- they are then on their way to becoming mere **Flat mates**.

4. DISTANCE IN MARRIAGE (STALEMATE)

The next stage in the progression is distance. If you are single, you are probably reading this chapter and thinking, 'My story will not be like this.' I hope so. But, the truth is that for most couples, unless one is intentional about enriching his or her marriage, a drift is natural. A marriage left untended leads to a physical or emotional distance between spouses. This state is like a **Stalemate. Stalemate** is a terminology in chess whereby there's no movement - one can't go forward or backward; you have to remain on the same spot.

At this stage, couples are spent from fighting and arguing, instead they keep their thoughts and your feelings to themselves and from their spouse. The tendency is to think that there is really no point talking to each other.

They may continue to do household chores together, washing the dishes or watching the TV together but life seems to be a drag cloaked in silence and a chilly distance. In the past they would share eagerly with each other as they got back home "Guess what happened at work?" or "…so and so said this" or "this is the way I feel right now". But now they may feel talking is either going to lead to an argument or that their spouse will merely grunt and keep reading the newspaper, surfing the net or flicking the channels. The resolve to not share with the spouse could be so strong that one party is struggling at work or with health issues and doesn't communicate it to the other party. I and my wife watched a sitcom where a lady went through a battery of tests that confirmed she had cancer without mentioning it to her husband whom she was becoming slowly but surely estranged from.

If only someone would break the silence, but often pride and hurt feelings prevent this. Sometimes they don't even go to bed at the same time. One partner comes back late to avoid having to talk to his spouse or buries his face in the computer when he is home. The only common thing they share is that they live in the same house. They're like two ships passing each other at night. All they see at night is their spouses back light.

5. Division in Marriage (Cellmates)

A couple distanced from each other will sooner or later, unless there's an intervention, move into disconnection or division. Many couples are at this point. Their lives are so dissonant; they are so out of synch which each other that they have become virtual strangers. They live in the same house but really have nothing to say to each other except things to do with the children. Often they live different lives, and it's at this stage that a spouse may say "I found out that we are no longer compatible" or 'we no longer have anything in common".

A divided couple feel like **Cell mates**. They are frustrated by the inability to move ahead in their marriage. They are compelled by marriage to live in the same house and feel like prisoners; sometimes they spend half the time looking outside the "jail house" window, wondering what life is like on the outside.

6. DIVORCE IN MARRIAGE (CHECKMATE)

The last stage is divorce and I am not even talking about going to the courts yet. Many marriages are in a state of emotional divorce right now. Many couples stay married for reasons other than love for their spouse. For many the only reason why they are still married is the children. Others are only stalling because of the financial cost to them in alimony or what members of the extended family will say. For the latter group, the only reason why they are still married is because it would be a taboo to members of their family or people in their culture to hear that somebody from their family or clan got divorced. They hold on and endure.

But oftentimes the silence becomes too loud, the chill too cold and when one of the spouses envisions another 40 years imprisonment with hard labour, he or she decides to checkout and then you've got **checkmate!**

My prayer is that what has been described in this chapter will help you to see what makes a marriage degenerate and that you will use this knowledge to diagnose where you are in your marriage and resolve to ensure that you do whatever it takes to make sure your marriage is one that endures. In chapter seven we will begin to look at how to achieve this, but first lets look at an issue that often proves to be the final nail in the coffin for many marriages.

CHAPTER 6

ARE YOU SUSCEPTIBLE TO AN EXTRA-MARITAL AFFAIR?

The possibility of an extra-marital affair is something few couples are willing to think about, much less talk about. Many will probably want to skip this chapter, thinking 'This doesn't apply to me…' I believe anyone who thinks that way is in denial and is not being honest. This is because one can only really speak of ones own convictions and resolve in the marriage- the truth is that you cannot be sure where your partner is at. You cannot speak with full certainty about how susceptible or vulnerable your partner may be to an affair. The best intentioned people do have affairs; many are caught off guard – having drifted into an emotional affair which then progress into a full-blown sexual affair. Good people do bad things at times of weakness. That is why the scriptures says "… let him who thinks he stands take heed lest he falls." It is actually wise not to make assumptions.

In this chapter we will be looking at what makes a person vulnerable to an affair. Let's start with a definition

"First of all you can only speak of your own convictions and resolve in the marriage. You cannot speak with full certainty about your partner's spiritual, moral or emotional state at any time. Even good people can sometimes do bad things."

WHAT IS AN AFFAIR?

An Affair happens when a person decides to meet their legitimate emotional love needs through another person other than exclusively through their spouse. **in an article titled 'What Is The Difference Between An Emotional Affair And A Physical Affair?', Cathy Meyer states**

An emotional affair is defined as any infidelity that occurs through feeling or thought. With the technological development of cell phones and the internet, the definition of cheating has been expanded to include the traditional definition, plus the feelings and/or thoughts that comprise emotional infidelity. Cheating now includes having intimate correspondence with someone while on a cell phone, meeting someone over the Internet and maintaining a close, personal relationship with someone other than your spouse. While it is healthy and normal for people to have friendships outside the marriage with men and women, an emotional affair threatens the emotional bond between spouses. Friendships are based on attraction, in that we are drawn to various qualities of our friends. Healthy friendships and attractions don't need to threaten a marriage at all, but add richness and enjoyment to life. When an attraction turns into an obsession or into an affair, it can become harmful to everyone involved and nothing is more harmful to a marriage than the breakdown of the emotional bond marital partners have for each other.

"An Affair happens when a person decides to meet their legitimate emotional love needs through another person other than exclusively through their spouse."

IS YOUR MARRIAGE STARVED OF AFFECTION?

Just as an individual who is starved of food or water for many days can do desperate and unethical things in order to satisfy his hunger or quench his thirst, a person who has been starved of affection and emotional connection could yield to the temptation to meet his or her need inappropriately.

29 "So is he who goes in to his neighbour's wife; Whoever touches her shall not be innocent.

*30 People do not despise a thief if he **steals** to **satisfy himself** when he is **starving**.*

31 Yet when he is found, he must restore sevenfold; He may have to give up all the substance of his house.

*32 **Whoever commits adultery** with a woman lacks understanding; He who does so destroys his own soul"* (Prov. 6:29-32 *NKJV*).

"Just as an individual who is starved of food or water for many days can do desperate and unethical things in order to satisfy his hunger or quench his thirst, a person who has been starved of affection and emotional connection could yield to temptation"

The above scripture makes it clear that regardless of the prevailing circumstances in a marriage, yielding to adultery to satisfy ones appetites is not excusable and has harsh consequences; nevertheless it also highlights an understanding of how it can happen – because of a hunger (in this scripture for food, in many marriages for lack of marital satisfaction or indiscipline and immaturity). God made all of us with legitimate needs of emotional and sexual intimacy that should be met only in a biblically appropriate way- within the confines of a marriage. Nevertheless, when it is not being met in marriage, people sometimes look for it outside, consciously or unconsciously.

"Regardless of the prevailing circumstances in a marriage, yielding to satisfy your appetites illegitimately is not excusable."

THE DANGER OF NOT MEETING EACH OTHER'S NEEDS IN MARRIAGE

A married couple could live in the same house, drive in the same car daily to and from work, sit at the same dinner table and sleep on the same bed with everything appearing normal externally. Yet deep inside there may be an estrangement or distance from their partner whom they long to connect with emotionally. Human beings are made for love and intimacy- we need to feel and show love, to know we matter and are significant to somebody. Love is so important that research has shown that physically frail babies, who aren't held, touched and shown love physically are less likely to survive than other babies like them who are showered with affection and care. When we are not loved we wither, life has less joy and often less purpose and meaning.

"Cathy Meyer states that An emotional affair is defined as any infidelity that occurs through feeling or thought. Cheating now includes having intimate correspondence with someone while on a cell phone & meeting someone over the Internet"

The thirst for love is such, that if the desire for it is not met we actively begin to seek it out. In many marriages the demands of a busy life, can mean that we neglect our spouses - we work late, don't make time to go out together, to talk or even to make love. If a spouse complains of neglect repeatedly but feels it falls on deaf ears, such a person can be vulnerable to yielding to the temptation of satisfying the love need through someone else who is willing and available.

SIGNS & SYMPTOMS OF AN EMOTIONALLY STARVED MARRIAGE

You can tell when a marriage is emotionally starved and heading for an affair. Perhaps one or some of the following echoes the thoughts of your heart.

"She lives her life without consideration for me. You would think we weren't married."

"He is never there for me when I need him the most."

"I feel down because I feel alone and abandoned by my spouse."

"My spouse and I no longer enjoy each other's company."

"I need to be touched by my partner in a way that he has never done before."

"The only time he talks to me or shows affection to me is when he wants sex."

"The only time she has sex with me is when she is craving my attention."

SO ARE YOU LIVING IN A LOVELESS MARRIAGE?

Stormie Omartian in her book titled "Praying through the Deeper issues of Marriage" states: When a husband or wife feels lonely, disconnected, distanced, disappointed or abandoned emotionally by their spouse, all it takes is being around someone who gives them a strong sense of being understood, acknowledged, or cared about. They are vulnerable and this can establish a connection with that person. Even if there is no physical infidelity, there is an infidelity of the heart that occurs that is not pleasing to God (Matt 15:19).

She says, *do you realize husbands that every time you are rude, critical, demeaning, verbally abusive, cruel, neglectful or abandoning of your wife that you create in her a fertile ground into which seeds of unfaithfulness can be planted? Unless she is extremely strong in the Lord, deep longings and thoughts will come to her heart and she can become ripe for an affair of the heart, if not the body. It's amazing how attractive someone else can look to you when the person who is supposed to love you no longer acts as though he does…*

Do you realize wives that every time you criticise your husband in a demeaning way, put him down in front of others, neglect to compliment him and let him know that he is valuable to you, or refuse to have sex with him that you make it much more difficult for him to resist the temptations that are everywhere around him? He is more susceptible to flattery and unholy attention than he would have been otherwise.

(Also read my book "Sex & Seduction Exposed" for more detailed information on the same topic).

THE PROCESS TO AN AFFAIR
WRONG CLIMATE

As previously stated, affairs tend to happen in a climate where there has been a season of drifting from one's spouse - when there is emotional distance due to neglecting each other and their needs. It also thrives where there are criticisms and feelings of not being valued by the partner.

WRONG SOIL

The propensity towards an affair builds as the heart is made vulnerable by the prevailing climate described above. It primes the heart of the affection-starved spouse into a state of dissatisfaction, resentment, bitterness and sometimes even feelings of hatred.

Dr. Harley, Jr., ref states that your emotions do not simply encourage you to be with those who make you happy - they also discourage you from being with those who make you unhappy. Whenever you associate someone with bad feelings, withdrawals are made from your Love Bank. And if more is withdrawn than is deposited, a Love Bank balance can fall below zero. When that happens the "Love Bank" turns into the "Hate Bank". When a person has a moderate negative balance with you, you will dislike them; but if the balance falls below the hate threshold, you will hate the person. Many people are living with spouses they hate!

When hate comes into the picture, your emotions are doing everything they can to get you out of there - and an affair or divorce is are logical ways to escape.

WRONG SEEDS

The wrong climate and soil then become fertile ground for wrong seeds to be sown into. Wrong seeds are thoughtful texts, flattering compliments or helpful deeds sent, made or done by an associate, friend or any other person of the opposite sex. It could be a work colleague, a boss in the office, an in-law or even a co-labourer at church. These actions which would be insignificant to someone in a strong marriage can have deep meaning for a person who is feeling emotionally neglected or is even beginning to hate their spouse. These words and actions can fasten onto their heart because they have been starved of them from their spouse. Furthermore, the proximity of the new love giver and the amount of time that is spent together often legitimately, for example, at work or in church facilitates the frequent occurrence of these love giving activities which can quickly cement the connection between these two people.

The most dangerous thing about this process is that oftentimes the connection between a spouse and the love giver develops innocently. It is sometimes possible for an attachment to have developed before either party becomes fully aware of what is going on.

> "Affairs usually start innocently, usually with an attraction to someone you know fairly well, someone with whom you spend time with each week by reason of work, family relationships or even planning church programmes"

WRONG HARVEST

The plot can quickly progress from an innocent friendship to a full blown sexual relationship. It will usually start with a stray thought or warm feelings which if meditated and acted upon can grow into a harvest of emotional entanglements leading to physical adultery and sometimes divorce.

(Also read my book "Sex & Seduction Exposed" for more detailed information on the topic of the Process of Seduction.)

The list below shows how relationships can develop from innocent into dangerously passionate liaisons.

THE ROMANTIC ATTRACTION SCALE

1) Repulsion – a negative feeling towards a person
2) Nothing – a neutral feeling towards someone
3) Acquaintance – a fleeting encounter with someone
4) Working Relationship – a relationship centred around tasks or roles
5) Friendship – a relationship based on commonality and shared interests
6) Chemistry– a relationship where there is physical attraction
7) Emotional Connection – a relationship based on deep understanding and acceptance
8) Romantic feelings – a relationship that involves sentiment, emotion, or desire that causes a person to indulge in fanciful thoughts or daydreams about another
9) Falling in Love – a relationship where the feelings for the other person are all consuming
10) Soul tie – a relationship based where the two people are deeply tied to one another

Oftentimes a relationship will start at level four which will create a base for interaction where common interests are discovered (level five). Many relationships will stay at this level but in some relationships attraction (level six) or an incident in which the two people share something deep and are helped by the other through it (level seven) can create the platform for an adulterous affair; especially if one or both parties are emotionally or physically vulnerable.

The list below also shows how quickly a relationship can move from mild attraction to a full blown sexual affair. You can measure where you might be by this scale.

TEMPTATION TO ADULTERY SCALE

1. Attraction –feeling drawn to another person
2. Temptation – a desire to act on an attraction
3. Emotional Connection - (Romantic feelings & thoughts)
4. Flirting
5. Verbally Expressing Affection
6. Sharing exclusive time (being alone together)
7. Holding hands
8. Kissing
9. Heavy Petting
10. Sexual Intercourse

If any married person is experiencing anything above level five in the romance to attraction scale and above level two in the temptation to adultery stage, with someone other than their spouse they are in dangerous territory. Serious and urgent thought and action needs to be taken to get out of the web of adultery and to salvage the existing marriage.

PART THREE

THE PLEASURES OF MARRIAGE

HOW TO ALWAYS ENJOY BEING MARRIED

CHAPTER 7

BACK-TO-SCHOOL

(DO YOU KNOW WHAT KEEPS LOVE ALIVE IN MARRIAGE?)

A lot of couples live life stuck on the cyle of disappointment and busyness. They still long for the fantasy - they pine for the dream mate, and each time they meet the reality of their spouse their disappointment deepens. They think or say to each other, 'you are not the way you used to be anymore.' That's because he was never like that and she was never like that - when you were dating, you each put your best foot forwaed. So you only saw the best parts of one another. That, in conjunction with the hormones released in the falling in love state caused you to be blinded to or to overlook the flaws or your partner. Many couples are also too busy to put in the work that will change their marriage; they want a good marriage, but they don't want to have to work at it. They haven't discovered the key to enjoying their marriage.

The key to enjoying your marriage or taking monotony out of monogamy is getting back to school. The Back-to-school stage is where you decide that instead of being disappointed and pining for a fantasy marriage, you are going to adapt and work at creating the kind of marriage you desire. When you are at this point you say 'In this marriage and concerning this person, I'm a novice. Now, who is this person really and how can I get the best out of them?' You decide to become a student of your spouse - to get to know them and what makes them tick. You ask your spouse, 'Who are you? What do you want? What are your likes and dislikes?' The back-to-school phase is the place where you begin to understand that you and your spouse are different and that you speak different languages and have different needs. As someone said, it sometimes feels as if men are from Mars and women are from Venus. For a long time I used to think women were a mystery (I still think so sometimes!). The Bible says that he that speaks in unknown tongues – 1 Corinthians 7:.. speaks not unto men but unto God. A part of me used to think women spoke in an unknown tongue many times. If the same is true for you need to ask God for the gift of interpretation of your own spouse's tongues so that you can have a Holy Ghost party in your house. Its hard work. Are you prepared to put in the work required to create a heaven on earth marriage?

I heard an interesting story about a lady who went with her husband to the hospital. They discovered that he had an illness which could be terminal. His wife decided to talk to the doctor alone to find out if there was anything she could do to help him get well. The doctor told her "If you don't want your husband to die you really have to be committed to serving him". She wanted to know how and he explained.

"This disease is so severe that in order to keep him alive you have to basically do everything for him so that all his energy can be conserved for getting well. It means you will have to wake up early in the morning to make a nutritious breakfast for him and take it to him in bed. All hot drinks have to be served at a certain temperature. You will also need to bathe him daily. Once a day take him for a walk in his wheelchair but make sure he's wrapped up warm. At home you can try and distract him from the pain by getting him to watch his favourite programs on TV or by reading to him. Let him have time with the children but make sure they don't wear him out. After you put the kids to bed in the evening, make him a light but nutritious meal and give him a massage and rock him till he goes to sleep. Is that clear?". The wife said "Yes doctor" and left. When she returned to her husband, he noticed that she was rather quiet and asked her, "What did the doctor say?". She replied, "The doctor said you are going to die." Put simply, she wasn't prepared to do what was required to keep her husband alive.

ARE YOU READY TO DIE?

Are you prepared to do what it takes to keep your marriage alive? A lot of us have come to the conclusion that there's no way in this world that we are going to do this or that. The secret to turning around a bad marriage is either to kill your spouse or kill yourself. I hope the first is not an option you are considering and regarding the second option, I hope you know that I mean killing the flesh, not committing suicide. My marriage gets better each time I come to the point where I count myself dead.

Galatians 2:20 says, 'I am crucified with Christ; nevertheless I live.

It is not I that live but Christ that lives through me.' You will experience heaven on earth in your marriage when you become like Christ to your spouse. That becomes possible when you realise that it's not about you enjoying heaven on earth, but about you doing what you can to make your marital home heavenly for your partner. When you create a heavenly experience, you may soon find that they are doing the same for you.

To be Christ like is to be loving. The bible says God is love (1 John 4:8), and those in Him have love and give love. Galatians 5:13 says ' through love serve one another'. That is the secret or the key to a successful marriage. When both spouses realise that marriage is a ministry, and that the emphasis is on serving one's spouse and not having our needs met- then we are on track. It's a heavy revelation and it can take time for it to fully dawn. It's important to know and understand what love is. Even children know what love means.

> "In the honeymoon stage and phase, there's no payment of bills. When you get back to your home, you see a pile of letters waiting for you: the gas, electricity, and water bills; and then, a note from the bailiffs."

UNDERSTANDING LOVE

A survey was done with some little children and the question they were asked is *What does love mean to you?*. This is what they had to say about love.

Billy, age 4: "When someone loves you the way they say your name is different."

Carl, age 5: "Love is when a girl puts on perfume and a boy puts on shaving cologne, and they go out and smell each other."

Danny, age 7: "Love is when my mommy makes coffee for my daddy and she takes a sip before giving it to him to make sure that it tastes okay."

Bobby, age 5: "Love is what is in the room with you at Christmas if you stop opening presents and listen."

Noel, age 7: "Love is when you tell a guy you like his shirt, and then he wears it every day."

Tommy, age 6: "Love is like a little old woman and a little old man who are still friends even after they know each other so well."

May, age 5: "Love is when mommy gives daddy the best piece of the chicken."

Chris, age 8: "Love is when mommy says daddy is smelly and sweaty and still says he's handsomer than Robert Redford."

Jessica, age 8: "You really shouldn't say I love you unless you mean it, but if you mean it you should say it a lot. People forget."

Rebecca, age 8: "When my grandmother got arthritis she couldn't bend over and paint her toenails anymore, so my grandfather does it for her all the time even when his hands have got arthritis too. That's love."

So what is love to you? You may have your own definition of love, according to scripture there are three kinds of love. There is eros, phileo and agape

"Noel, age 7: "Love is when you tell a guy you like his shirt, and then he wears it every day."

EROS

Eros is romantic love or sexual love; it's a love based on sexual desire or attraction. Eros is about looking into each other's eyes and relishing that sparkle in the other person's eyes. It is about romantic, candle-lit dinners and the lingering touch. Its about the rush when the other person touches you and the desire you feel for them. This is what attracts many people into marriage; but many soon find out that it is ephemeral. To have an expectation of this kind of love throughout married life is not realistic. If you desire to enjoy eros in your marriage, it does not come naturally you have to recreate it. We'll talk later in this chapter and also in the next chapter about how to do this.

"Tommy, age 6: "Love is like a little old woman and a little old man who are still friends even after they know each other so well."

PHILEO

This is friendly or brotherly love - based on shared interests, commonalites and affinity. While many marriages are initiatied by eros, they need phileo to sustain them. Phileo is enjoying each other's company and going out on walks together. It is going shopping or to the movies together. It is having mutually-engaging conversations. A couple with eros and no phileo will find marriage hard work indeed! After the feeling of being in love and the sexual rush have worn off, they may find they have little to talk about or enjoy together. That is why it is foolhardy to make a lifelong choice solely on feelings and attraction.

> "Love is staying there all the way – and that can sometimes be a difficult one. Love is loving your wife or your husband even when they gain weight. It is loving your spouse even when they've sinned against you. It is God's kind of love."

Many people don't understand why the church discourages sex before marriage and a lot of Christians engage in premarital sex. I used to lose sleep over it in the past but I don't anymore; I now know some people choose (through their disobedience of scriptural guidelines) to learn life lessons the hard way. One of the things that keeps a marriage together is friendship. When two people say they want to get married, I ask some simple questions that show whether they are friends or not. If they are friends, when all of the excitement of falling in love is gone, they'll still be able to look at each other and enjoy each other's company. That's Phileo.

And then, it is when both of you can remember and laugh at your foolishness in the past. Phileo is also feeling lonely when your spouse is away on a trip.

"You need to come to terms with the fact that marriage is not 50/50. It is 100%-0% sometimes"

AGAPE

The highest kind of love is agape. This is a sacrificial or committed love. It is a love that is unconditional and is not dependent on the worth of the object of love. It is the kind of love that endures and that holds on during tough times and seasons. Some people have told me, "You are blessed, you have a good wife." I say "Yes I do, but you know what? I am also married to a human being like you." Our marriage is not a gift from God. Nobody is 'blessed with a good marriage.' You have to make a good marriage happen. As much as I love my wife we have our differences and disagreements but I made a decision to be married to her.   There is no such thing as divorce in my dictionary and my wife knows it. When the storms come, I know in my heart that, sooner or later they will pass away, and I am prepared to sit out the storm with the help of God. That's the mindset of agape love- its prepared to hold on no matter what.

" Our marriage is not a gift from God. Nobody is 'blessed with a good marriage.' You make a good marriage happen."

T.D. Jakes shares an inspirational story about the early years of his marriage. In the first weeks of his marriage, his wife had an accident and broke her hips. She couldn't walk and was wheelchair bound for a while. He had to carry her around and the doctors said she might never walk again. It was a long and painful process whilst she learnt to walk again and regained the normal capacity to do life. Think about what it must have been like for him. Any expectations of frequent sex would have been seriously comprised and his needs would have had to go on the back burner as he assumed the role of 24 hour nurse. That's agape love.

Agape love is loving your spouse even when he or she is not loving or when he or she does not look lovely. Agape love is loving your wife or your husband even when they gain weight. Agape love is definitely not waiting until your partner is perfect before you love them. It is loving your spouse even when they've sinned against you. It is God's kind of love. The Bible says while we were yet sinners, God loved us- Romans 5:8.

I have found over the years that any woman can fall in love, but it takes a real woman to stay in love. Any man can sleep indiscriminately with different women (all he needs is a believable, sugar-coated tongue), but it takes a real man to sleep with the same woman for 40 years and keep her sexually fulfilled and happy.

"If your marriage is not working anymore, it's because you left it to chance. Marriage requires work. It will work if you work it."

WORK WITH WHAT YOU'VE GOT

Perhaps the most important key to transforming a marriage is accepting your spouse as he or she is and being willing to work with what you've got. Are you ready to accept your spouse, warts and all, with his or her imperfections? If you are not, you are not yet willing to accept the principle of agape love which is what can turn your marriage around. But if you are, then you are saying ' Lord, this is what I've got, please help me to make something out of it'.

The account of the wedding at Cana of Galilee in John chapter 2 shows the importance of weddings and the marriage institution to God, and His power to transform ordinary things into something special. Jesus performed his first miracle at that wedding. I find it interesting that when Jesus was asked to provide wine, Jesus needed something to work with - He asked for pots of water to be filled and that was what he turned to wine. Fill your pots with water first: Jesus was saying, 'You bring your own ingredients first. Bring what you have and I will turn it into wine.'

"Have fun. It's easy to get rather boring and stiff. Bring some fun into your home."

Many times couples come for marriage counselling not because they want to work at their marriage, but because they want an expert to confirm that their marriage is beyond repair, they want a certificate of death pronounced on their marriage by someone in the know. The wife comes to counselling saying, "I don't love him anymore" and the husband is also saying, "I don't feel the way I felt about her when I first got married to her." That's ok, but are you willing to work at it? Are you willing to bring your water for Jesus to transform to wine? If your marriage has turned from wine to water and you want Jesus to help you, bring your water at least. But if you come without water or without a pot, without an willingness to work at it – the prognosis is not good.

I know it's not always easy, sometimes there has been so much hurt and so much pain; but are you willing to step out once more in faith? Many times to make a marriage better you will have to push beyond feeling and act on command. You may not feel loving or sacrificial or giving towards your spouse, and you may not feel like working on your marriage. But are you willing to do something to build your marriage despite how you feel? Mary told the servants in John 2: , 'Anything He asks you to do, do it.' The first step in a turnaround is usually acting on a command - the servants may not have felt like filling the pots with water, but if they didn't they wouldn't have had wine. You have to ask yourself, not 'What do I feel like doing in this situation?' but rather 'What is the godly response in this situation? What would God have me do?' . To heal a broken marriage you must lean on God's directive and do what He would want rather than what you feel.

"In order to bring the spice back, you need to become the wife of his youth again. Many husbands have to shut their eyes to remember the wife of their youth."

Marriage is not 50/50, it is sometimes 100%-0%. Sometimes one person in the marriage is not contributing anything, whilst thats not's right, that's life. In that case it's just the other party holding up the marriage, and this is ok if (although understandably this can be wearisome over a long period). If you can hold on, God can do something. Read on as we discover how to turn a dis-satisying marriage experience into an intoxicating one.

CHAPTER 8

THE LITTLE THINGS THAT KEEP LOVE ALIVE IN MARRIAGE

(HOW TO TAKE MONOTONY OUT OF MONOGAMY)

HAVE YOU GOT A WATER OR WINE-FILLED MARRIAGE?

One of the ways the scriptures describe the sparkle or the romance in marriage is the illustration and the symbolism of wine. A marriage where the husband is endeared to his wife, and where he is romantically disposed to his wife and vice versa can be likened to rich wine. On the other hand, a marriage in which the man or the woman treats the spouse just like a brother or sister is one where the wine has gone flat or has turned into water. What is the difference between wine and water? We need to understand this symbolism so as to understand the difference between monotony and monogamy.

> ## "It was God's intention to make marriage a monogamous institution, but it was never His intention to make it monotonous."

WHAT IS MONOGAMY?

Monogamy is defined as 'the practice or condition of being married to only one person at a time.' God made marriage to be monogamous. It was God's intention to make marriage a monogamous institution, but it was never His intention to make it monotonous.

What is monotony? Monotony is wearisome uniformity or lack of variety. Just as you wouldn't enjoy listening to a song sung only in one tone, a marriage with no variety is dull.

MARRIAGE IN MULTI-COLOUR

It is important to have colour, variety and texture in every marriage. Life was never meant to be lived in a monotonous sequence. God wants our marital lives to be colourful like wine. Wine in a glass is red and attractive; its pleasing to the eye and is fragrant to smell. It is very different from water. While water is essential for everyday activites like drinking, bathing and washing, it is colourless and bland. When its time to celebrate people break out a bottle of wine, not water; because wine is sparkling and intoxicating. It promises excitement, laughter and joy. In a dating relationship, you find that the individuals are intoxicated with each other; they are "drunk with love". Sadly though many marriages have lost that sparkle. Is it possible to regain it? The answer is yes, you can do so firstly by prioritising, and introducing variety into, your marriage and by re-igniting love in your spouse.

> *Let your fountain be blessed, and rejoice in the wife of your youth, a lovely deer, a graceful doe. Let her breasts fill you at all times with delight; be intoxicated□ always in her love.* Proverbs 5:18-19

Turning water into wine

1. Create routine dates with your spouse.

The challenges and the vicissitudes of life can easily pull marriage partners apart, so you need to be intentional about investing time in your marriage. If you don't, its easy for your spouse to feel that other things are more important to you than him or her. A good marriage doesn't happen by chance, you have to create it. I'm a very busy man and I enjoy what I do its very easy to get sidelined. I have to be intentional about letting my priorities be reflected in my use of time.

My desire that in my life God be first, my spouse next and then my children before work and other activities is something I constantly strive to live out. Before I book appointments outside, I schedule time with my wife. At the beginning of the year when I plan my diary I block out time for family holidays, key events in the childrens diary and general family time. I need to do that so that I can be with them and enjoy them, if I don't, my diary gets blocked up and the people I love are neglected. Every quarter, I try to get away with my wife. We love old cities so we visit different cities when we get a chance. We have one evening a week which is our evening – in this time we sometimes go out and have a meal together, just to reconnect or if either of us is too tired, we stay at home and watch a movie together, eat ice cream and have a laugh. Its wonderfully restorative.

Water is colourless. It is nice and it will quench your thirst but you see, wine symbolises celebration. Wine is also flavoured. Water is flavourless. Wine many times has a sparkle to it. Wine in a glass is inviting and enticing, but water is bland. "

2. CONNECT WITH YOUR SPOUSE DAILY.

Its really important to make an effort to keep in touch with whats going on in your spouse's life – to find out whats on their mind, how things are at work, in their friendships or family relationships and what their current concerns are. You do this mainly by talking regularly and daily if possible.

I used to be guilty of not doing this. She would ask me, 'So how was your day today?' and I would reply, 'Fine.'

"So what happened today?" she would say.

"Nothing" I would reply.

It was only when my child started doing the same thing to me, that I understood how frustrating and limiting it could be.

"How was school today?" I would ask my son.

"Fine" he would say.

"What did you do today?" I would ask.

"Nothing" he would say.

In frustration I would finally retort, "Come here. Do you think I'm paying all that money for you to do nothing? Tell me, what did you do today?". Only then would he tell me about the classes he attended or remember something a teacher said to him.

After this happening a few time, I began to teach myself. I realised that it wasn't fair to go back home with 'nothing' or 'fine' as a standard reply to most questions about my day. Now, I get a notebook to write what I do in the day so I don't just breeze through the day and forget what I did like most people. I go over the list when I'm going home so that when my wife asks me what I did, I have plenty to say. It's an effort but its so worth it. I want to know whats going on in her life and I want her to know whats going on in mine- that's how intimacy is created in marriage.

3. DEVELOP A COMMON INTEREST.

My wife and I love to go to bookstores, we like to spend hours browsing and eventually selecting one or two books to purchase. Sometimes we take our children, and they too have developed a love of books. Afterwards we eat at a restaurant and have a good time enjoying each other. We also love property. We visit every development that opens up near our home and see what they're building; we keep up with property trends and prices and we visit historical homes. We just enjoy it. It's a great way to spend time together-sharing something we both enjoy. What could you and your spouse enjoy together? We know couples who share an interest in football, in art and in politics. Is there a sport, activity, interest or hobby you could enjoy together? You will find it enormously enriching for your marriage.

4. HAVE FUN.

It's easy to get boring and stiff and only do routine stuff. Bring some fun into your home. I love to tease my wife, crack jokes and invent crazy dance moves; she often rolls her eyes but she tells me she loves it. My wife has a few fun things she loves to do with the kids too. She teaches them 80's dance moves and has even been known to challenge them to a race through the mall (which I am proud to say she won, thankfully there were no parishioners nearby to observe their pastor's wife tearing through Lakeside shopping centre)! One of the things we particularly enjoy is embarrassing our kids- it gives us great pleasure! They cringe every time we sing in public or kiss each other, so we do it often. The important thing is that laughter is frequent in our home, we want our house to be a joyous place and we work to make it so.

5. BE CREATIVE IN BED.

Make a commitment to meet each other's sexual needs regularly, whether it's convenient or not. Sometimes life can be so busy that you need to schedule to have sex in marriage. Don't be afraid to do so, anything that's important needs to be planned. And when you do have it, be creative. Read the Songs of Solomon and you will see that God designed sex to be varied, fulfilling and exciting, not monotonous. Many husbands don't know it is in the bible and many wives think it's the only book there! One such woman sent a note to her husband on their anniversary. It was from Songs of Solomon 7:11. It says, "Come my beloved, let us go down to the countryside. Let us lodge in the villages. There I will give you my love." What a woman! She planned for a new place to make love, she was explicit about her desire for her husband, and she created anticipation. I bet he turned up early!

Now that we have talked about some practical things you can do to begin to stir variety and interest into your life, lets look more closely at how to reignite the feeling of love in your marriage.

GETTING YOUR SPOUSE TO FALL AND REMAIN IN LOVE WITH YOU
(THE PRINCIPLE OF EMOTIONAL NEEDS)

The mystery of how to reignite love was solved for me when I began to understand the principle of emotional needs, the importance of meeting them and how meeting or not meeting them impacts a marriage.

Over many years of working with couples, I have studied various materials and found that though various authors use different terminology to describe what they are trying to say, they are essentially saying the same thing. Many writers on the topic of marriage and love all agree that the key to sustaining a marital relationship long-term is ensuring that both parties feel loved and valued in the marriage. Perhaps more than any emotion the feeling of loving and being loved is one that we all crave. Although love can be fleeting, its power cannot be denied. Kings have been known to abdicate thrones because of the intensity of their feelings for another, Generals have lost wars because they were "love sick" and secret agents have divulged national secrets because they were in love. If one could somehow learn what it takes to ignite that emotion and sustain it, then happier and longer marriages are guaranteed. The key to doing this, it appears, is meeting the emotional needs of one's spouse.

"The human emotions although often described as fleeting are very strong.Kings have been known to abdicate thrones because of the intensity of their feelings for another, Generals have lost wars because they were "love sick" and Secret agents have been found to have divulged national secrets because they were in love"

LOVE LANGUAGES, LOVE TANKS & EMOTIONAL BANK ACCOUNTS

Though writers are agreed on the power of the human emotions and the need to have them met by one's spouse, they describe them in different ways. Some authors describe every human as having **an Emotional Love Tank** like a car's fuel tank that regularly needs to be filled up with fuel in order to function like it ought to. Others like Dr. Willard F. Harley, Jr. illustrates the same principle using the term **Emotional Love Bank Account** in which one's spouse needs to make regular deposits and fewer withdrawals in order to avoid the sad state of being emotionally overdrawn or bankrupt. Author Gary Chapman calls meeting your spouse's emotional needs **speaking their Love Language.**

WHAT IS AN EMOTIONAL NEED?

According to Dr. Willard F. Harley, Jr., an emotional need is a craving that when not satisfied, leaves you with a feeling of unhappiness and frustration. He describes how emotional needs and the love bank work to create feelings of love in the excerpt below.

Within each of us is a Love Bank that keeps track of the way each person treats us. Everyone we know has an account and the things they do either deposit or withdraw love units from their accounts. It's your emotions' way of encouraging you to be with those who make you happy. When you associate someone with good feelings, deposits are made into that person's account in your Love Bank. And when the Love Bank reaches a certain level of deposits (the romantic love threshold), the feeling of love is triggered. As long as your Love Bank balance remains above that threshold, you will experience the feeling of love. But when it falls below that threshold, you will lose that feeling. You will like anyone with a balance above zero, but you will only be in love with someone whose balance is above the love threshold.

"According to Dr. Willard F. Harley, Jr., An Emotional need is a craving that when not satisfied, leaves you with a feeling of unhappiness and frustration. "

When our most important emotional needs are being met by our partners there is the feeling of "in love-ness" or we "fall in love." When they are not met we "fall out of love." At this time couples are emotionally obsessed with each other. They tend to believe and see the person they have fallen in love with as perfect and tend to ignore their faults. A lot of time is spent doing things that add credit into the partners love bank- things like paying compliments, buying cards and gifts, doing recreational activities together or acts of service for each other. This is the state in which many dating couples rush into marriage and run off to sign the dotted lines, ignoring advice and warning signals or signs that are obvious to all others. This feeling is usually soon lost in marriage when the hard realities of life begin to creep in and choke out the amount of time spent together. As daily responsibilities, chores, bills, children and irritating habits all begin to show up and the management of them involves negative responses or behaviour from the spouse this causes massive withdrawals in their love banks which leads them into the eventual feeling of falling "out of love."

"Daily responsibilities, chores, bills, children, irritating habits all begin to show up and these things begin to tip the partners into times of irritation, snapping and so on which begin to cause massive withdrawals in their love banks which leads them into the eventual feeling of falling "out of love."

Gary Chapman ask's 'Could it be that deep inside hurting couples is an "emotional love tank" with its gauge on empty? Could the misbehaviour, withdrawal, harsh words and critical spirit occur because of that empty love tank?'

"This feeling of "in love-ness" can also be stimulated and maintained no matter how long the couple have been married for if they keep making love deposits into each other's Love Banks or Tanks."

MEETING YOUR PARTNER'S LOVE NEEDS

This feeling of "in loveness" need not run out though, it can be stimulated and maintained no matter how long the couple have been married for if they keep making love deposits into each other's Love banks or tanks.

When we first meet a person falling in love is not real love (some call it "Puppy love" or infatuation) because it is not a deliberate decision, and is often motivated by attraction or the 'newness' of the relationship. However in marriage there has to be a conscious choice to keep the love in the relationship alive and sometimes a deliberate effort through sacrifice to make it happen. We usually wonder where that lovey-dovey feeling has gone, but hardly are able to recognise that it only disappeared because we no longer put in the time to pursue, nurture and cultivate our partners like we used to. Our marriage and spouse has been ticked off our lifetime to-do list, and replaced with work deadlines, children, bills, the general busyness and other realities of life that such that we don't have or put in the time and energy required to fan the flame of passion whose embers are slowly dying away. Since time and effort put in at the beginning of the relationship is what caused the romantic sparks to fly and be ignited in the first place, the same ingredients if carefully and deliberately applied can help recreate that romantic atmosphere again.

"To rebuild this much desired romantic climate in marriage, couples need to schedule time alone with each other daily, where they give each other focused and undivided attention..."

To rebuild the much desired romantic climate in marriage, couples need to schedule time alone with each other daily, in which they give each other undivided attention and just focus on meeting each other's most felt emotional needs. At this time couples must ensure that they do not say or do anything that hurts or offends the other person. It has to be a time when only the positives are built in and reinforced.

> "Since time and effort put in at the beginning of the relationship is what caused the romantic sparks to fly and be ignited in the first place, the same ingredients if carefully and deliberately applied can help recreate that romantic atmosphere again."

Having established that love can be reignited by deliberate action and focused time, what are some of the practical things and actions we can do to fill our spouses love tank?

> "When our most important emotional needs are being met by our partners there is the feeling of "in loveness" or we "fall in love.""

SPEAKING YOUR PARTNERS LOVE LANGUAGE

Gary Chapman in his book "The Five Love Languages" gives five broad categories of things we can do to fill our spouses love bank or how we can speak their love language.

> # When they are not met we "fall out of love." At this time we are emotionally obsessed with each other."

He believes that when your spouse's emotional love tank is full because you understand and make efforts to speak his or her language he or she feels secure in your love, the whole world looks bright and he or she feels empowered to fulfil his or her potential. Although every individual appreciates when any of the five love languages are demonstrated to him, he will feel particularly fulfilled and touched on their "sweet spot" when one or two of the five which mean the most to him are demonstrated in a special way. The five love languages are:

1. Words of Affirmation
2. Quality Time
3. Receiving Gifts
4. Acts of Service
5. Physical Touch

Before we talk in more depth about love languages, I'd like to take a short detour into unmet childhood needs.

UNMET CHILD HOOD NEEDS

It is worth noting that some spouses have very deep emotional needs which they are sometimes desperate to have met due to deficiency's in their childhood and upbringing. This further complicates issues within the person's marriage. Gary Chapman says that Child Psychologists affirm that every child has certain basic emotional needs that must be met if he or she is to be emotionally stable.

> *Among those emotional needs, none is more basic than the need for love and affection, the need to sense that he or she belongs and is wanted. With an adequate supply of love the child will develop into a responsible adult. Without that love he or she will be emotionally retarded... When a child really feels loved, he will develop normally but when the Love tank is empty, the child will misbehave. Much of the misbehaviour of children is motivated by the cravings of an empty 'Love tank'.*

"Many parents were able to provide for their children's physical needs but were not aware of the corresponding need to meet their children's emotional needs."

How will you know if your spouse has unmet needs that spring from childhood issues? Is your partner very shy or insecure, or very outspoken and brash, or a perfectionist or highly competitive? Talk to them about it and try and explore the roots of these traits. If these issues are rooted in childhood events and mired in issues of worth and acceptance with parents. Many parents were able to provide for their children's physical needs but were not aware of the corresponding need to meet their children's emotional needs. If you have a partner who is has deep emotional needs due to childhood issues then you can help to build what was lacking in their childhood validation or affirmation, by liberal and consistent doses of love credit into their emotional account.

USING THE FIVE LOVE LANGUAGES TO FILL YOUR SPOUSES LOVE TANK

You may be asking 'How will I know which one or two of the five love languages are my spouses primary love language?'. The key is to ask which one does he or she show the most to you. This is because we often give love the way we expect or desire to recieve it. A person who pays a lot of compliments or say's ' I love you' or ' I value you' often, will often desire to hear it. It is likely that their love language is acts of affirmation. Of course, you could take the guesswork out of it and just ask your spouse. As you identify your spouses love language, take the time to begin to do some of the things outlined in the section describing their love language below, in order to fill your partners love tank.

WORDS OF AFFIRMATION

As highlighted above, the person who has words of affirmation as their primary love language will like to hear words that are uplifting, encouraging and affirming on a regular basis. If a man keeps saying, " That woman really respects her husband, look how she talks about him', his primary love language could be words of affirmation.

Such a person will appreciate
- Being told that you love them
- Compliments about their looks, appearance or achievements
- Cards or letters filled with expressions of love

QUALITY TIME

The person who has words of affirmation as their primary love language has their love time filled by regular time alone with their spouse doing things that encourage emotional connection such as talking or simply being together. If a wife keeps saying, "You don't spend time with me", her primary love language is quality time.

Such a person will appreciate
- Time set apart to be with them
- Outings where you can be alone with them
- Evenings at home spent together (without the TV or radio on)
- Holidays where there is plenty of time to do things together as a couple

RECEIVING GIFTS

The person who has receiving gifts as their primary love language loves to receive gifts as it makes them feel valued. They will especially like gifts that show thought or care or special knowledge of them. Gifts do not have to be expensive to be meaningful. If a man gushes over a gift and keeps saying, " I feel so valued by the sacrifice you made to get me this" his primary love language could be receiving gifts.

Such a person will appreciate

- Thoughtful gifts such as a framed picture of the two of you or the children or something monogrammed.
- Little gifts on a regular basis – a hand picked flower, a notebook or a keyring.
- A gift to do with a hobby the person enjoys e.g. a golf club or tennis racquet.
- Significant gifts on birthdays or anniversaries.

ACTS OF SERVICE

The person who has acts of service as their primary love language appreciates it when you do things to help them out, to serve them or to relieve their burdens or responsibilities. They will especially appreciate actions that show you understand the demands on them and that you care to share their burdens. If a wife keeps saying, "You never help me out around the house" her primary love language could be acts of service.

Such a person will appreciate

- You volunteering to run errands for them e.g. pick up or drop a child at school, pick up dry cleaning or do grocery shopping.
- A significant time saving device such as a dishwasher (a great gift for a housewife with this love language). Don't buy this as a birthday or anniversary gift though; instead arrange for it to be delivered on a regular day of the week to show you care to relieve her burden.
- You insisting they spend a morning or afternoon in bed to rest.

PHYSICAL TOUCH

The person who has physical touch as their primary love language loves to be touched. They feel loved when they are touched and stroked. Women who have this love language appreciate non sexual touch; but the men who have this love language love non sexual and sexual touch. If a man frequently touches and kisses his wife, it is likely his primary love language is physical touch.

Such a person will appreciate
- Frequent hugs and cuddles.
- A rub on the shoulder or waist as you pass each other in the hallway or kitchen.
- Having their hands held, especially in public.
- Frequent back rubs and massage

WHAT MEN AND WOMEN WANT FROM EACH OTHER

Whilst Gary Chapman presents the meeting of love needs in a gender neutral way, based on activites and services enumerated above; Dr Willard Harley, Jr., illustrates meeting emotional needs on a gender specific basis. He states that though these needs are common to both male and female alike, the first five are usually more suited to men's emotional desires and cravings, and the last five are more complementary to women's needs.

MALE

1. Admiration
Being respected, valued and appreciated clearly and often by their spouse.

2. Physical Attractiveness
Having a spouse that is physically fit with and wears hair and clothing in a way that that is attractive and tasteful to him.

3. Sexual fulfilment
Sexual experience that brings out a predictably enjoyable sexual response in both of you and that is frequent enough for both of you.

4. Domestic support
Creation of a home environment that offers a refuge from the stresses of life; including management of the home and care of the children (including but not limited to cooking meals, washing dishes, washing and ironing clothes and house cleaning).

5. Recreational Companionship
Developing interest in her spouse's favourite recreational activities, learning to be proficient in them, and joining in those activities with her spouse.

FEMALE

6. Conversation
Talking about events of the day, personal feelings, and plans for the future; showing interest in her favourite topics of conversation;

balancing conversation; using it to inform, investigate, and understand her and giving her undivided attention.

7. Affection

The expression of love in words, cards, gifts, hugs, kisses, and courtesies; and creating an environment that clearly and repeatedly expresses love.

8. Financial Support

The provision of financial resources to house, feed, and clothe the family at a standard of living acceptable to her, but avoiding travel and working hours that are unacceptable to you.

9. Family Commitment

Scheduling sufficient time and energy for the moral and educational development of your children; including reading to them, taking them on frequent outings, developing the skill in appropriate child-training methods and discussing those methods with her. Also avoiding any child-training methods or disciplinary action that does not have her enthusiastic support.

10. Honesty & Openness

Revealing positive and negative feelings, talking about events of the past, daily events an plans for the future. It also includes not leaving a false impression and answering questions truthfully and completely.

In the final two chapters we will look at these and other key needs of men and women in fuller detail.

CHAPTER 9

WHAT DO MEN REALLY WANT IN A WIFE?

If you desire to succeed at married life you have to ask the question, "What kind of wife or husband does my spouse really want" rather than the more popular question "What do I really want in a spouse?". It is important to know what you want so as to make the right choice in a partner but it is even more important to know what your partner really wants so that you can be the right partner to them. This is the secret to success in business. Businesses that succeed are the ones that ask their customers the right questions on a regular basis and go ahead to develop products and services to meet those needs.

I asked a group I started on Facebook called "Inspiration by Dr.Sola Fola-Alade" the above question. The group has about 3,300 members to date. Below is the summary of the thoughts of the respondents. I believe the thoughts are representative of what men want in a wife. Of course every individual man will have their own peculiar needs. Make some little improvements in your marriage based on what you learn from the list below and you will see a big difference in your marriage. You can see the efforts you make as little gifts of love to your spouse.

1. MEN WANT AN ATTRACTIVE WOMAN WHO MAKES AN EFFORT AT LOOKING GREAT, KEEPS IN SHAPE AND CARRIES HERSELF WELL

This point is very important. I want to underscore this because men face temptations daily. This is why I have chosen to deal with this first. Of course women face temptations too but in a different way.

We live in a society that bombards men daily with images, because it understands that men are visual beings. When you ride on the train, every other advert has a naked woman on it. It's the same when you get on the internet. When my son was 6 years old, he was playing on the computer when the image of a naked couple kissing came on the screen. Using computer language these images tend to corrupt the male "internal processor" and eventually destroy his 'hard drive', but the drive is relentless

.

The same thing happens on the television and in the office, his secretary is possibly scantily dressed. Todays man is constantly being offered various sexual temptations - he has a menu of these things on offer, like a buffet.

However at home it's a different story. At home he only has a set meal (i.e. is his wife). Whilst I don't want to put any woman under pressure, I think every wife has to work hard to ensure that the set meal is more attractive than the buffet being offered outside. Don't just give your man plain quaker oats. If you understand that your husband has been exposed to rice risotto, spicy chicken ala carte and beBeef stroganoff, when he gets home you had better give him some exotic meal! I am sure you get the point.

I recommend giving your husband the gift of attraction. I mean things like being watchful of your weight and dressing. If the man married you as a size 10 and you are now a size 16, whilst its understandable that childbirth and raising children will affect your figure, if he doesn't like it, don't ignore it. If your husband starts dropping hints like "Let's register at the gym' or 'What do you think about buying a treadmill in the house?' or ' We eat too much fat in this house and its showing" I pray you get the point. Instead of asking, "So what do you think?" when you wear something that is really one size smaller than you are with the hope that you might just fit in it today, decide to do something about it. Some men have to close their eyes to remember the wife of their youth- you don't want that!

One more thing, its important to work at being attractive to your man, not all men. If everybody else compliments you about your dressing and your husband still complains, please listen to your spouse. You are not married to everybody else. If you husband likes yellow and you like black, then do consider wearing yellow. Marriage does not succeed on doing what is comfortable for us but rather on doing what pleases our spouse.

2. MEN WANT A WOMAN WHO WILL GIVE THEM GREAT LOVE I.E. CONSISTENT, FREQUENT AND PASSIONATE LOVE MAKING

Give him the gift of sex. Many women will not consider sex as a gift because the experience of sex for a man is different from sex in a woman's experience. Women's sexual response is different from that of men. Some people say men are like gas cookers. You turn on the gas and you hear a fast gushing sound, immediately, a combusting flame appears. Men don't need much to motivate them sexually. On the other hand, a woman has to be prepared and put in the mood for what is going to happen at night. So women are said to be like electric cookers, they take time to get started but when they are hot, it takes them some time to simmer. So women expect and require the process of foreplay that leads up to sex. They don't just want it, they need it. Good sex in marriage requires time and consideration, be willing to give it.

Unfortunately many women are not open to sex because their men are selfish in their approach to sex (either out of ignorance or self-centredness) and end up leaving their women sexually frustrated. Many women see sex as a chore, I even heard that one woman said to her husband "Please hurry up and get it over and done with it". It's a big shame because such women do not experience the release, satisfaction and fulfilment in marital sex that God designed. There is a big difference between having sex and making love. When two people have sex without real intimacy it may satisfy the flesh at the time but it's like sending a letter, closing up the envelope, putting the stamp on and sending it off without placing the letter in it. It feels empty. Having sex is really just an exchange of bodily fluids. Making love however involves intimacy, emotional connection and a knitting of two souls together, as well as physical satisfaction.

> "Many men are selfish in their approach to sex (either out of ignorance or self-centredness), and they end up leaving their women sexually frustrated. "

Whilst I encourage women to be sexually available to their husbands I also want to encourage the time to become better sexual lovers. If you can, attend one of our Marriage Enrichment Weekends (we have a session dedicated to this), read Christian books on sex (there are many on this) to learn technique and give plenty of time to emotional connection and foreplay with your wife. If you do this, I can assure you that the quality of your sex life will improve and your wife will desire you sexually like never before.

3. MEN WANT A WOMAN WHO SUPPORTS THEIR VISION

Women should give their husband the gift of incubation. This means that a woman should show excitement when her husband shares his dream. It is a sorry sight whenever a man tells his wife, "You know what? I've got this idea, when we get a little money, we'll buy a house" and she looks at him thinking, "What about the last project you said you'd do? What money do you want to use? You haven't even returned the last amount of money you borrowed yet. You're just a dreamer."

If you want to make your husband feel like a king, when he says, "I have a dream" (like Martin Luther King) please do sit down and listen intently. Ask him what you can do to make this dream a reality and then go ahead and do what you can. That's all a man needs. Even if you don't initially feel like it, please do it. These are the little things that will make a big difference in your marriage.

4. MEN WANT A WOMAN WHO BOOSTS THEIR CONFIDENCE & ENCOURAGES THEM WHEN THEY ARE DOWN

Give your husband the gift of encouragement. In today's society, men are under constant pressure. Even the mere thought of getting married can bring much pressure as a single man. When I was getting married, my wife called me on the mobile phone when we were approaching the church for the wedding ceremony. She asked, 'How are you feeling?', I said I was fine. Then I overheard her father who was seated beside her telling her, "Ah, Sola must be feeling the weight and pressure of getting married now. I can hear the tension in his voice." What he said was very true because I had a lump in my throat. My designation was about to change in the next few minutes. At the time, I could barely even support myself, I was just managing to pay my own bills and now I was going to carry the added responsibility of looking after a wife.

On the whole men are easy to take care of, they just need a hair cut and a shave every week or two, but women are another ballgame. They need to perm or straighten or weave their hair, they need pedicures and manicure and facials. They need different clothes for different outings, they need high heels and flats and hats for weddings. They need sanitary products and toe dividers for when they paint their toenails. It appears to men that women's needs are endless and expensive! Many men are anxious about their ability to provide for their wife and family.

Whilst women carry the pressure of caring for the children and household, the man faces the pressure of providing for the children and household. The man may not help you with doing the dishes like you would love him to, but be rest assured that he is agonising about how he's going to deal with the unpaid mortgage balance.

> "The man may not help you with doing the dishes like you would love him to, but when they think of the unpaid mortgage, they face intense psychological pressure. They also they feel a pressure to be like the Joneses."

Men are also under constant pressure to perform at work and to measure up with friends. If his friend drives a Jeep while he drives a Fiat Punto, you can be sure its an issue for him unless he's extremely secure. Many women don't understand this. Women are under pressure to conform while men are under pressure to perform because we live in a world that measures their worth by their achievement or net worth. Men face intense psychological pressure, so he really does need your encouragement. When he comes back home and he's not talking, please be patient. If God were to open your eyes you would literally see smoke coming out of his ears.

"She opens her mouth with wisdom. And on her tongue is the law of kindness" (Proverbs 31:26 *NKJV*).

A woman's mouth is one of her most powerful weapons. With her mouth a woman can build up her husband and make him feel like a king or she can cut and reduce him to a crumb of bread. Believe me, your man needs your encouragement.

5. MEN WANT WOMEN WHO LISTEN AND TREAT THEM WITH RESPECT

Give your man the gift of honour and admiration. Men are wired differently from women. While women need appreciation, a man needs admiration.

What do I mean by admiration? Admiration is almost synonymous to adoration. Men need an atmosphere of respect, praise and admiration to function effectively. Check out the man who is going through serious problems at work; perhaps a man who the boss is criticising or who is not meeting his work targets. Such a man is a disoriented man. If he gets back home to meet a woman nagging about undone household chores, he is likely to react negatively. However if that man comes home and hears his wise wife say things like, "There is no one like you, thanks for working so hard to look after us", it rebuilds him and recharges his batteries. By the following morning, he is ready to take on the world again!

"One of the things that still leaves me puzzled , is how two people who were so in love with each other and were excited at the thought of seeing each before they got married, can degenerate to the point where at the very least become bored with themselves and have to endure each other's company later in marriage."

The Amplified Bible in Ephesians 5:22 says, "Wives, be subject (or be submissive and adaptable) to your own husbands as a service to the Lord." Verse 33b says, "And let the wives see that she respects and reverences her husband." That implies noticing him, which means it's possible not to notice your husband when he walks into the room. It continues by saying she should make sure, "She regards him and honours him and prefers him and venerates him, esteems him; and that she defers to him, and praises and loves and admires him exceedingly."

"But if that man comes home and hears her say things like, "There is no one like you," and she begins to commend his good attributes, it rebuilds him and recharges his batteries. By the following morning, he is ready to take on the world! "

It is interesting that the Amplified Bible uses about ten different words to describe the way a woman should treat her man. That shows it is important. Just as a fish needs water, a man needs praise and admiration. When Abigail met David in the book of 1 Samuel 25 even though he was not a king yet; she said, "May all your enemies die before you even get near them." She told him, "There is nobody like you. When you enter into your kingdom remember me, oh great one." I'm not saying you should call your husband the great one, but you can tell him, "You are my hero. I like the way you do the things you do." Find your own creative way of praising and admiring him, he'll be putty in your hands.

6. MEN WANT A WOMAN WHO CAN COOK FOR THEM AND TAKE CARE OF THE FAMILY AND THE HOME

Men need the gift of domestic care and support. In recent times, there has been a lot of talk about the modern man who stays at home to look after the baby and the house while the wife goes off to work. In reality many such arrangements have problems. Most men would still prefer their wives look after the home front and offer them domestic support. I realise that in today's world things may not always fit this pattern but it is often the expectation.

While I encourage married men to be domestically involved and to share in household chores especially if their wives work outside the home, I know that a well kept home and well cooked meals makes many men feel well looked after and cared for. It's important to talk about this as a couple and agree a compromise that works well for both of you.

7. MEN WANT A FUN AND EXCITING WOMAN WHO IS INTERESTED IN THEIR HOBBIES

Men want recreation and *productive* conversations with their wives. Note the word *productive*. When women give gifts, they tend to give gifts that are nice and beautiful but not necessarily functional, whilst men tend to give functional but not beautiful gifts. This tells us a lot about how men and women approach conversation. Women tend to enjoy the whole process of the conversation, including little details about how the day went and they don't mind meandering conversations. Men tend to be headliners; if the conversation is not going towards an objective they tend to switch off. I believe men should learn to converse with their wives on their own terms, but it is also helpful for every woman to know how men converse and for both parties to stretch at conversing in a way that's meaningful to the other.

Men also enjoy recreational companionship. They love it when their wives either enjoy their hobbies with them, or at least enjoy talking about their favourite football teams or golf tournaments. Whether you support his team or the opposing one, just get into it with him and enjoy it together.

8. MEN WANT A SUBMISSIVE, UNDERSTANDING AND NON-NAGGING WIFE

Give your husband the gift of submission. Submission is from two words, 'sub' which means 'under' and 'mission' which refers to 'assignment'. Put together, it means bringing your mission underneath or under your husband's own. When a woman gets married, she changes her name, her address and her status. It is a sign of submission. Submission is a very subtle weapon and wise women know it. Sometimes, it can be used by women to get what they want.

A man who does not know God can also won over by his wife's submission to God. That is why 1 Peter 3:7 recommends a meek and gentle spirit.

> "Submission is a very subtle weapon and wise women know it. Sometimes, it can even be used by women to get what they want. A man who does not know God can also won over by your own submission to God. "

A woman can submit to her husband by listening to him, taking his view into account in decision making, making choices that honor him, speaking respectfully to him, speaking well of him to others, looking for ways to serve him and make him happy.

If wives could take the above advice to heart and apply them daily to their marriage they will truly find that it is the little things that make a big difference in a marriage.

CHAPTER 10

WHAT DO WOMEN REALLY WANT IN A HUSBAND?

I have found that a lot of men do not know how to treat women as they should be treated. This is because of wrong societal mindsets concerning women. Unfortunately, in some parts of Africa, the Middle East, and some other developing countries, women are seen as personal property. In some of these cultures and religions, one man is equivalent to five women. The women are seen as little more than domestic slaves, meant to be seen and not heard. In other places like the western world, they are seen as sexual objects due to the proliferation of pornography and prostitution. In my opinion, pornography is not just about sex, it's about the degradation of women.

Many men have been trained to think that women were just made for sex, for cooking, cleaning, child bearing and child rearing. If that is your notion, you need a brain wash.

SOME MEN NEED A BRAIN WASH

Whenever you see a particular thing, person or project constantly under the attack and scrutiny of the enemy, that thing must be important to God. When Moses was born, the Pharaoh tried to kill every child of his age. When Jesus was born, King Herod tried to kill every child within his age range. In the same way ever since humanity was made, Satan has tried to destroy women and womanhood. I strongly believe this is because they are God's secret weapon in this end time.

> "Whenever you see a particular thing, person or project constantly under the attack and scrutiny of the enemy, that thing must be important to God. "

I want to announce to you that the female species is the pinnacle of God's creation. God created the woman after the man. The best usually is kept to the last.

WHY DO MEN TREAT WOMEN LIKE TRASH?

Apart from the societal ills I mentioned above, a lot of men inherited wrong mindsets from their fathers about women. We don't just inherit property and money; people also inherit the way their fathers treated their wives. When a man does not have any regard for women, there is a high likelihood that his dad did not have any regard for his mother. A lot of men who don't provide for their wives had fathers who did not provide for their mothers. Their fathers have told them, "Hey son, put the woman in her place. If she misbehaves, give her a good beating and she'll behave!". A lot of us need to unlearn what we have been taught about women and learn how best to treat them.

"I want to announce to you that the female species is one of the greatest creatures that God ever made. God created the woman after the man. The best usually is kept to the last."

In order to properly deal with the subject of how women want to be treated and what women really want in a man, I conducted a survey on my Facebook group and the the issues women ranked as most important are listed below. In this chapter I have used excerpts from some of my wife's messages to illustrate the points.

1. WOMEN WANT A MAN WHO WILL TAKE THE TIME TO UNDERSTAND HIS WOMAN

In the same way you married men should live considerably with your wives, with an intelligent recognition of the marriage relationship- 1 Peter 3:

BFA: 'Don't just assume that you can get married and have a successful relationship. You need to approach it intelligently and actually take on the responsibility of understanding your wife. Take the time to study and understand your woman. Many men feel their wife is like an alien to them. They think she's very peculiar, strange and quite different from them. It is true and you should appreciate that difference. Her nature as a woman is different from yours, so please do not treat her as you would treat another man! The Bible says that women are the 'weaker vessels'. What the Bible is saying is that women are physically more fragile than men and their constitution is different from men. Every man needs to understand this.

It is commonly acknowledged that women are more emotional and intuitive than men. Recognise and accommodate this. The fact that women are more emotionally intuitive means they read people and situations better and they sense and observe things that men don't. That explains why a woman will tell her husband, 'Your secretary fancies you' and the man will respond saying 'That girl? No way!' But she can tell. She simply knows! Women are better at picking up emotional and non-concrete things than men are. One of the other things that get men wound up sometimes is the fact that women cry easily. It's the way she's wired, it's different for you. She enjoys a good cry, don't always take it personally.

"The fact that women are more emotionally intuitive means they read people and situations better and they sense and observe things that men don't."

Sometimes it's hard for women to be as focused, determined and visionary as men are, because we are carers and our desire to care for people means our energies are often dissipated. That's why God put us together. He puts one person who able to look far ahead and aim for the shot (men) with someone who is detailed and oriented, who is able to keep a lot of things going (women). This is why it is important to accept each other, appreciate these differences and harness them.

There's an advantage that the differences we have can play, and a wise man needs to know that about his wife, appreciate it and value it.'

2. WOMEN WANT A HUSBAND WHO PRIORITISES THE FAMILY, BECAUSE WOMEN NEED FINANCIAL AND RELATIONAL SECURITY

BFA: 'Security is very important to a woman, especially financial security. I was doing research online and found that single working women buy homes at twice the rate of single working men, even though single working men earn twice the wages of single working women. This confirms that women are very security prone. When interviewed they affirm that they are looking for a nest; somewhere they can call home, somewhere that's theirs. This is why some women have earned a reputation as gold-diggers.

However, I do think that a man's earning capacity is one of the things a woman should consider when she's marrying him. He might not be rolling in money but he needs to be able to support his family. Research also shows that women are more risk averse than men, that's why husbands and wives squabble over the use of spare money, whether to save it or invest it. The woman is more likely to save it after putting some away for a shopping spree while the man is more likely to use it in business.

She wants herself and children to be number one in your life - not work. Many times when men tell their wives, 'I'm working all these hours to make money for you...' It's not really true! You are doing it because you want to be big; you want to be cool and drive a big car, you want to make a statement, so don't make your family an excuse. They want you and not the big car, so please cut your hours.

"However, I do think that a man's earning capacity is one of the things a woman should consider when she's marrying him. He might not be rolling in money but he needs to be able to support his family."

There was a certain couple we were counselling, the husband was very ambitious and into a lot of businesses, but his marriage was falling apart. The wife called us because she was frustrated. Eventually, we met with them. Whilst we were talking, my husband asked him, 'Let's fast forward into the future. If you become mega rich, would you be happy to enjoy the money by yourself?' The man said no. 'Would you still want your wife and kids to be around then?' my husband asked. The man said yes. We helped him to see that he needed to slow down. What the woman was saying was that he could not continue at that pace and keep her happy. By the time he had made all the money he wanted, she would have left out of frustration.

"A lot of women feel they are in competition with their mothers-in-law. Be wise in the way you relate with your wife and your mother."

Your wife wants to be Number One in your life without having to compete with any other thing or person - and that includes your mother. A lot of women feel they are in competition with their mothers-in-law. Be wise in the way you relate with your wife and your mother. Don't let them be in competition. Though special and important to you, your mother is no longer number one; your wife is. A lady told me that after she got married her mother in-law was very sweet to her but once the husband was not around, she made it clear she was the first and would always be. The wife replied by reminding her mother-in-law that she would still be around long after she was gone! Maybe that wasn't particularly a wise thing to say, but it is a good picture of the battle that is on.

Another way to show that your family is important to you is to prioritise family events in your calendar. Block out certain dates i.e. your wife's birthday, wedding anniversary, and your children's birthdays and make out time on those days. Those are the things that matter to women. Don't wait till you receive a call from your wife's sister, reminding you to call your wife and wish her happy birthday or anniversary. Don't further compound issues by bringing home a half-dead flower picked up at the filling station on the way home. What she wants is that as she wakes up on the day, you'll sing to her, hug her and kiss her. As she descends the stairs, if she finds different flowers on each stair level- you've made her day, no year! That's what she's looking for. Make breakfast for her. When she gets to work surprise her with a box of chocolates on arrival... Be romantic and blow her mind - that's what she wants.

Also make plans for the family. A lady told us that her husband had done a budget forecast for the family till 2015! Now that's a man that planning for his family's future. Be involved in their lives. Someone said she told her husband that he really needed to help their son with his homework. The man came back from work, placed the son in front of a computer and said, 'Okay, start working.' That's not helping with the homework. Sit down with them and talk it through with them. Research shows that boys whose fathers get involved with their school work, do better because the man is the authority figure. My son just gained entrance into the best school in Essex and we paid in blood, tears and a lot of shouting; but when his dad says "son, turn that game off and pick your book," no challenge is put up at all! Get involved in your children's live. All these things help your wife know that she's Number One in your life.'

3. WOMEN WANT AN AFFECTIONATE AND ROMANTIC MAN WHO WILL SAY NICE THINGS TO, PURSUE AND SPEND TIME WITH HIS WOMAN

BFA: ' A woman needs to feel special to her husband or significant other. Tell her she is special to you; tell her "I love you", "I appreciate you" and compliment her regularly. Don't let the only compliments she hears be those from her work mate or her boss. It's easy to take your wife for granted because you see her day in day out, but its important not to' .

"A woman needs to feel special to you, her husband or significant other. Tell her she is special to you; tell her "I love you", "I appreciate you" and compliment her regularly... It's easy to take your wife for granted because you see her day in day out, but this is very important."

You also need to discover her love language. You need to know what gets your wife wired and practise it regularly. The second part of 1 **Peter 3:7** says you give **honour to wife as a weaker vessel and treat her with respect**. The word HONOUR means to pay money, to value, and to esteem as precious. You probably know already that if you have a wife, you will spend a bit of money on her hairdo, clothing and other basic needs, but what that scripture is saying is that you should lavish praise on your wife. Value your wife, honour her and esteem her.

GIVE HER YOUR UNDIVIDED ATTENTION

BFA: 'One other thing that is important to a woman is undivided time with you. She doesn't want to compete for your attention with the newspaper or sports. On your night out, don't get engrossed in reading a paper or ask her to watch football with you. That's not bonding, unless you both enjoy football.

"She doesn't want to compete for your attention with the newspaper or sports. On your night out, don't get engrossed in reading a paper or asking her to watch football with you. That's not bonding, unless you both enjoy football. "

A woman once told her husband that on her birthday, she wanted him to take her somewhere nice and he agreed. On the said day, he got quite busy, so he sent his driver to give her some money to go to the restaurant by herself. He felt that was a perfectly legitimate thing to do. Since he couldn't make it, she could go and he would pay. There was a massive link missing however: HIM. She could have gone to dinner by herself anytime she wanted; it's the communion with him that was important to her. One of the things you can really do to make your wife appreciate you is to spend time with her in a place where there are no distractions.

My husband has emphasised the importance of talking in bed. In most people's bedrooms there are no distractions. The kids are in their rooms and even if there's a TV in the room, it usually isn't on. It's just the two of you and an unspoilt time to bond together. It's important as a couple that you plan connection time regularly, otherwise you can easily lose sight of each other. Plan weekends away at least twice a year.

When we have Marriage Enrichment Weekends, it always amazes me when people tell me it's the first time they've been alone together since they got married. It's not healthy. Try planning one evening a week alone as a couple. Put the kids to bed early and spend some time connecting.

Another thing that is very important to women is non-sexual touch. It's very important for a woman, that you can touch her, kiss her, hug her and hold her without wanting it to lead to full sex. I understand that this can sometimes be difficult for men. At one Marriage Enrichment Weekend, a man said, 'It's like saying you'll go to the shop, try on the clothes and not pay for it…' . That was how he saw touching without progressing to sex. But do you know a lot of women enjoy doing just that? They go to the shops, try clothes on and leave them! Try to honour your wife every now and then by taking the time to hold her, kiss her and not put pressure on her for sex.'

"Another thing that is very important to women is non-sexual touch. It's very important for a woman, that you can touch her, kiss her, hug her and hold her without wanting it to lead to full sex."

4. WOMEN WANT A KIND, CARING, GENEROUS AND TRUSTWORTHY MAN

BFA: ' One way of showing kindness and thoughtfulness is gifts. Some of the gifts that mean the most to me from my husband are not the expensive gifts. They are things like going to the stationery store to pick up notebooks for himself and picking up some for me in the feminine colours of the ones he got for himself. Or once when we went to Spain I saw an inexpensive necklace and earring set I liked but decided not to buy because I had spent quite a bit of money. I saw it again at duty free shop on departure and mentioned I liked them. Later on as we were preparing to board the plane he made some excuses about going to quickly pick something up. At the time, I was upset that he was going back to get something when we supposed to be boarding. Imagine my surprise when he gave me the gift later and I realised he delayed our plane boarding so that he could pick up the jewellery set. Little thoughtful gestures like that draw a woman's heart.'

Also relationally, the woman needs to feel secure in the relationship. She needs to feel that you only have eyes for her and that her position in your life is not threatened. That is why it's important to be accountable to your wife. Don't hide your mobile phone or your email. It is legitimate for a woman to question your trust if you are hiding your mobile and don't let her have the password to your email. I have come to so trust my husband that although I have his password, I never check his email. I have free access to his mobile but never check it because he has never given me any reason to doubt him. If he did I would check it and it would be right to do so because he's my partner and is accountable to me. If you've had an affair and slipped up before, then you have an extra duty to be accountable. That means if your mobile is asked for you should surrender it and that if access to your email is required, you should give it.

Trust is not assumed, especially after it has been destroyed. You can't say 'Just trust me' and expect it. It must be rebuilt by being open and accountable. As long as you are saying ' Trust me but don't check me, you are not serious'. You need to understand that relational security is a fundamental need for a woman. If she doesn't feel secure in the relationship, then you are in trouble because she will make your life hell. She will nag you, question you and query you.'

> "Trust is not assumed, especially after it has been destroyed. You can't say 'Just trust me' and expect it. It must be rebuilt by being open and accountable."

5. WOMEN WANT A MAN WHO IS FUN TO BE WITH, GREAT AT COMMUNICATING AND WHO WILL LISTEN WHEN HIS WOMAN TALKS

BFA: ' Women *need* to feel connected to the special person in their lives, and for a woman one of the main ways of connecting is through conversation. Men use words to simply convey facts and information, whereas for women words mean much more. They use it to convey words and information but also to explore and discover their thoughts and feelings, which helps them feel better. When a woman is upset, she just wants to talk to somebody and even if no solution comes up, she gets relief from just talking about it.

> "Women need to feel connected to the special person in their lives, and for a woman one of the main ways of connecting is through conversation."

Sometimes my sister will call from Nigeria and we'll talk for a while. At the end, I would feel as if steam has been let out and that I had released some tension. Later when my husband asks, 'So, what did you people talk about?' and I tell him 'Different things, just general gist…' He can't understand how you can talk for an hour and not have any concrete thing that you spoke about.

Ask a man what happened to him today and he'll tell you he went to work, he did this and that. A woman will tell you who she met at the bus stop, what she was wearing and what they discussed. Women love to go shopping. My husband still doesn't understand how you can spend a whole day in a shopping centre, and worse still, not come home with anything! Its like our conversation- we don't need to have a purpose for visiting, we just enjoy the process of browsing.

"Women need to express themselves and talk, and a wise man is the one who makes time to accommodate his wife to talk to him."

Women need to express themselves and talk, and a wise man is the one who makes time to accommodate his wife in conversation. A key factor which makes women vulnerable to affairs is when they have husbands who don't give them time to express their hearts. One of the biggest gifts you can give your wife is the gift of communication. Be available for her to talk with. She doesn't really need you to say much. Just let her talk: it's important to her.'

6. WOMEN WANT A MAN THAT IS SECURE IN HIMSELF, NOT DOMINEERING AND WHO RESPECTS AND APPRECIATES HIS WOMAN

BFA: 'Understand that women need respect too. Many times we've been told about how important it is for a woman to respect her husband, but a woman also needs to be respected by her husband. According to 1 Peter 3:7, we are heirs together. That means we are allotted something jointly or equally possess something or have equal entitlement to something.

> "Many subconsciously think women are a little bit less than men in their estimation or value but that is not biblical. You need to appreciate the role your wife plays in your life."

The world isn't about men living large and women serving them in order for men to be fulfilled. This scripture makes it clear that we are joint heirs, with equal entitlement to the fullness and goodness of life. That means your woman too deserves honour and respect as a joint heir with Christ. We are different but we are equal. It is important especially for people from African or Caribbean backgrounds to understand that the woman is not less than the man. Many subconsciously think women are a little bit less than men in their estimation or value but that is not biblical.

You need to appreciate the role your wife plays in your life. I think it is amazing to note that when God gives a man a wife, He is giving him the gift of a helper. I know how valuable a helper is because I recently got a personal assistant and I know how she has changed my life. I know the difference that comes from having someone to delegate things to. It allows me to fully or better exploit God's gifting in my life and I understand how critical she is in realising the things that God has called me to do.

This is the same role a woman plays in her husband's life and one of the ways you can appreciate her or value her is by how you treat her (and not just in the things you say). Go out of your way every now and then to buy her a gift; take time every now and then to compliment her and let her know you really appreciate what she is doing. Tell her, 'You are special to me and I couldn't be where I am without you. I acknowledge the role you have played in my life...'. It should also show in how you talk about her to other people and how you talk to her in front of other people.

When it comes to making decisions as a married man, if you really understand your wife to be a gift to you and someone who is key in helping you fulfil destiny, then you know that there are decisions you should not make without consulting her. There are virtues that God has put in her to help you make the right decisions. A wise man who wants his marriage to stand the test of time will take the time to involve his wife. Some men have a problem in this area because they feel their wives are not developed enough in a particular area. As a man, if you have a wife that you cannot consult, sit down with and trust to make valuable contributions when making important decisions, that is your fault. The Bible says the husband is supposed to wash the wife and present her, so you have a role as a man in developing your wife.

"One of the things that men don't understand these days is how much responsibilities women have. The juggling act that is a woman's life: from work, to children, to domestic duties, to paying bills, to family requirements, to church commitments, and to the extended family."

Before we got married my husband had told me, 'I am a Pastor and this the way of life that you can expect. There are things you will have to leave behind and there are some things you're going to need to develop. You are going to have to improve your prayer life and you may have to teach. There are also responsibilities you will have in church.'

It is your duty as a man to develop your wife. If you're a business man, you have a duty to carry your wife along and let her know what your business involves. School her so she can at least keep pace with you and be able to play her role in your life as your partner.

One of the things that men don't understand these days is how much responsibilities women have. The juggling act that is a woman's life: from work, to children, to domestic duties, to paying bills, to family requirements, to church commitments, and to the extended family. These are some of the various things she has to keep balancing.

As a man, you just wake up in the morning, dress up, pick up your briefcase and go off to work. Meanwhile the woman has to get the children and herself ready. She has to plan meals and cook the meals only for you to come home and say, 'Oh, no! Rice and stew again?' Sometimes, I see some married women and offer them spa vouchers because they look so tired and badly in need of a break. Once in a while you ought to do that. Tell your wife, 'Why don't you treat yourself for the day? Go and get a massage or a facial. Fix your nails too and I'll pay.' Or say, 'This weekend, why don't you spend the day with your friend? I'll take care of the kids.'

We service our cars every year. If you don't, one day it just packs up. You don't want your wife to fall ill. Whenever I have a little headache, my husband runs around the house asking if there is something or anything he can do to make me feel better. He does this because if I get ill, he will have to cook, do school runs and so on. So if you want an easy life, prevent your wife from breaking down- do maintenance and repairs regularly.'

7. WOMEN WANT A MAN THAT WILL ALLOW HIS WOMAN TO PURSUE HER DREAMS

BFA: ' You need to understand that your wife's life also needs to have impact. In *Genesis 1:28 God says "Let us make man in our own image and let them have dominion. "* God created both male and female to have dominion over all the earth, so your woman also has a desire to have dominion in an area. She wants to have an area in which she's making impact, where she's of consequence and in which she is significant.

"so your woman also has a desire to have dominion in an area. She wants to have an area in which she's making impact, where she's of consequence and in which she is significant."

When I got my personal assistant, I sat her down and asked her what are expectations were from the job and what her long-term aspirations are. I see her role as not only serving me but me helping her develop and getting something out of her role. I understand that life isn't only about me. She also has her goals and ambitions that she desires to express and fulfil. If I don't facilitate that, I would not be a good boss and I might end up losing her quickly, because her desire also have to be fulfilled.

I have had women confide in me, 'my husband won't let me work.' Or 'My husband has issues because I earn more than he does.' Your wife's pay cheque is irrelevant to her position in your life. The Bible says that the woman is the glory of the man. It gets at me when I see a man driving a Jeep, which can be so big it needs two parking spaces. You can hear the music, everything is sharp and the interior is cream and sparkling. Then you' see his wife in some old banger driving up behind him. The man is looking sharp while the woman is dragging three children along and looking like someone about to faint. When people see your wife, her state should speak well of you.

If your woman is flourishing, taking territory and using her gifting, it's to your glory and honour and it will bring certain things into your life. A lot of men say they want this but you will need to render the support required to make this happen. That means some adjustments need to be made in your life. If your wife is going to have a high flying career, maybe there are some domestic things you don't do now that you will have to do. There are some days you'll need to pick up the kids, days you'll need to load the dish-washer or serve the food she's cooked. If your woman is going to express fully what God has put in her, then you are going to need to make some adjustments to support it.'

SFA: 'Men also need to empower their wife. This is one area that a lot of men are found wanting. One person that really amazes me is Joyce Meyer. Each time I see her on TV and look back at what she used to be, I see how great her husband is. He was secure enough to release her into ministry and not tie her to a sink at home. As a result, she has become such a blessing to the whole world. Her husband was secure enough to say, 'You have a gift and I release you.' Unfortunately a lot of men are rather selfish. Because they have a vision of owning several houses in London and also want to go to business school, they tell their wives to stay at home. By using the phrase 'empowering her,' I mean women need to be encouraged to discover their purpose and fulfil their dreams. Sometimes what this entails is the husband sacrificing some of his own time and some of his own dreams so that she can become who she was born to be.'

8. WOMEN WANT A MAN WHO WILL PROTECT HIS WOMAN PHYSICALLY, SPIRITUALLY, EMOTIONALLY & MENTALLY

BFA: ' When managing the household finances, I sometimes get scared by the figures. On telling my husband, I expect him to enter my cocoon of worries with me but then he says 'It will be well, the money will come. We will do this or do that to get by…'; just reassuring me that all will be well. His taking the time to reassure me stops me from worrying and makes me feel protected'.

SFA: 'You need to protect your wife. Many women feel overwhelmed by the pressures of life: the children, home work, bills, issues, finances, having to clear up after you all the time, thinking for you sometimes and how to meet your physical and emotional needs.

You can protect her emotionally and mentally sometimes by supporting her domestically. Encourage her to take some time off to rest while you lend a hand at home, especially with the children. You can also protect her emotionally and mentally by talking to her, encouraging her and giving her plenty of non sexual touch especially back or leg rubs and massages – let her know you care and that she is not alone.

You can also protect by praying for her and your household. Don't let your wife be the main person labouring spiritually over your household. The bible says the man is the head of the home – it's your job to make sure they are protected, not hers.

EPILOGUE

In this book we've explored the dating and courtship phase before marriage, we have journeyed through the stages of a bad marriage and we have discovered the ingredients of a good one. If there are a few salient points to be taken it is this – good marriages require skill, effort and time.

Whatever you do – make time for each other

In his article titled "Summary of Basic Concepts of Love" Dr. Willard Harley, Jr. says:

Give your spouse your undivided attention a minimum of fifteen hours each week, using the time to meet the emotional needs of affection, conversation, recreational companionship and sexual fulfilment. This policy will help you avoid one of the most common mistakes in marriage - neglecting each other.

I suggest that you (a) spend time away from children and friends whenever you give each other your undivided attention; (b) use the time to meet the emotional needs of affection, conversation, recreational companionship, and sexual fulfillment; .... When you were dating, you gave each other this kind of attention and you fell in love. When people have affairs, they also give each other this kind of attention to keep their love for each other alive. Why should courtship and affairs be the only times love is created? Why can't it happen in marriage as well? It can, if you set aside time every week to give each other undivided attention.

Time alone away from all others has to be created to allow this to happen as the four needs mentioned here are best enjoyed and fostered when not shared with others but rather alone with one's partner. Women often resent having sex without conversation and affection first and men resent talking and being affectionate without any hope for sex and recreation. But when a husband creates time specifically to talk and show affection to his wife and she creates time specifically to enjoy recreational companionship and sexual intimacy with her husband – each spouse knows their spouse prioritises them, their needs are met, their love bank is filled and the much desired romance and feeling of love is restored into the union.

"Women often resent having sex without conversation and affection first and men resent talking and being affectionate without any hope for sex and recreation."

Here's to a joyful marriage – it will work if you work it!

BIBLIOGRAPHY

Chapman, Gary. *The Five Love Languages: How to Express Heartfelt Commitment to Your Mate (new edition)*. Northfield Press, 2004.

Harley, Willard F. Jr., *His Needs, Her Needs: Building an Affair-Proof Marriage.*
Baker Publishing Group, 2001.

Harley, Willard F. Jr., *Summary of Basic Concepts of Love.*
Available from www.marriagebuilders.com.

Omartian, Stormie. *Praying through the Deeper issues of Marriage*. Harvest House Publishers, 2007.

Meyer, Cathy. *What Is The Difference Between An Emotional Affair And A Physical Affair?* Available from www.about.com, 2008.

SOME OTHER PUBLICATIONS

BY DR SOLA FOLA-ALADE

21 WAYS TO MIND YOUR OWN BUSINESS (VOLUME 1)

SO WHO DO YOU REALLY THINK YOU ARE?

DISCOVER YOUR HIDDEN TREASURES

SEX & SEDUCTION EXPOSED
EXPOSING SEXUAL TRAITS

LEADERSHIP & LIFESTYLE MAGAZINE

Visit www.developingleaders.net

MARRIAGE CHECK UP

How Healthy is Your Marriage?

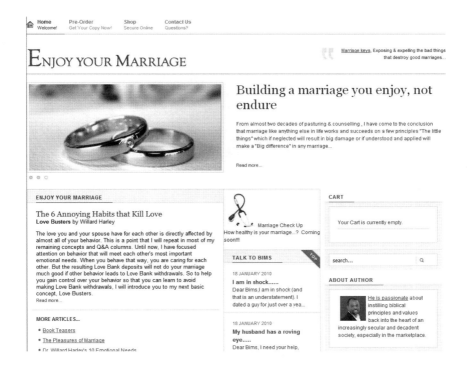